Thomas Speedy

Craigmillar and its Environs

with notices of the topography, natural history, and antiquities of the district

Thomas Speedy

Craigmillar and its Environs
with notices of the topography, natural history, and antiquities of the district

ISBN/EAN: 9783337181482

Printed in Europe, USA, Canada, Australia, Japan

Cover: Foto ©Andreas Hilbeck / pixelio.de

More available books at **www.hansebooks.com**

CRAIGMILLAR

AND ITS ENVIRONS

WITH NOTICES OF THE

TOPOGRAPHY, NATURAL HISTORY, AND ANTIQUITIES OF THE DISTRICT

BY

TOM SPEEDY

AUTHOR OF 'SPORT IN THE HIGHLANDS AND LOWLANDS OF SCOTLAND WITH ROD AND GUN'

WITH NUMEROUS ILLUSTRATIONS

SELKIRK: GEORGE LEWIS AND SON
MDCCCXCII

All Rights reserved

TO

SIR JAMES GARDINER BAIRD, Baronet,

WHO,

DURING A LONG RESIDENCE AT THE INCH,

BY HIS COURTESY AND KINDLINESS

ENDEARED HIMSELF TO ALL INTERESTED IN THE

WELLBEING OF THE DISTRICT.

𝔗𝔥𝔦𝔰 𝔚𝔬𝔯𝔨

IS RESPECTFULLY DEDICATED

PREFACE.

THE historical interest which for several centuries has attached to Craigmillar Castle and the surrounding landscape is my apology for the publication of the present work. Such a work, I felt persuaded, would be acceptable to many long familiar with the traditions of the district, as well as to a large number of those who from distant lands have made pilgrimages to the time-honoured castle. The work makes no pretensions to high literary culture, but it does claim to be a faithful and reliable record of the times, places, and circumstances to which it refers. The materials have been collected with much care, after a residence of many years on the Craigmillar estate. The advantages thus derived have been greatly increased, and my labour lightened, by the valuable aid which I have received from several competent authorities in their respective spheres. Among these I would specially mention Mr Thomas Ross, who has supplied me with valuable information regarding the architectural features of the ancient ruin. To several of my fellow-members of the Edinburgh Field Naturalists' Society I am also indebted—especially to Mr A. Moffat, Mr M. King, and Mr John Lindsay, for information regarding the botanical aspects of the district; and to Mr John A. Johnston for the geological features. To the librarians of the University and Signet Libraries and their courteous assistants I also owe my best thanks for the facilities afforded me in consulting old and rare books.

T. S.

THE INCH, EDINBURGH,
August 1892.

CONTENTS.

I.—THE CASTLE: ITS ARCHITECTURAL FEATURES.

PAGE

View from the battlements—Impregnable position of the castle—Successive alterations on original plan—A curious staircase—The Great Hall—"Queen Mary's Room"—The curtain walls of the castle—Skeleton found in dungeon—The towers of the castle—The living rooms—Ruins of the chapel—Arms carved on the walls 1

II.—THE CASTLE: ITS HISTORICAL ASSOCIATIONS.

Derivation of name—Notices in old records—Successive possessors—State tragedy enacted in castle—Its capture by the English—Its intimate connection with Queen Mary—A royal conference—Bothwell at Craigmillar—James VI. here plans his matrimonial tour to Denmark—Battle between the royalist and rebel forces Sir John Gilmour, proprietor of Craigmillar—Structural alterations made by him—His successors—The last tenants . . 24

III.—FAUNA OF THE DISTRICT.

Badgers—An otter hunt—A "run" with the Duke of Buccleuch's hounds—Story of a stoat—A bat's nest—A "meet" of the Mid-Lothian harriers—Trait of natural affection in a rat—Depredations of voles—Popular dread of "reptiles"—Hatching of newts and frogs—Fishing with a frog for bait—Fish of the district . 54

IV.—AVIFAUNA OF THE DISTRICT.

Rich variety of bird-life in Craigmillar district—The aquatic birds—The owl family—Adventure with a tawny owl—Crows and rooks—Story of a cuckoo—"Jacky," the Liberton magpie—Alarm raised from proceedings of a woodpecker—The thrushes and other song-birds—Diving feats of the little grebe—Incident regarding a sparrow-hawk—Food of the kestrel—Wholesale capture of the lark—Superstitious ideas regarding the lapwing—Gulls attacking sickly lambs—Velocity of flight in a pheasant—Do starlings devour larks' eggs?—The tits—The sedge-warbler's song—The smaller song-birds 80

V.—BOTANY OF THE DISTRICT.

Flora of Craigmillar district rich and varied—Flora of Arthur's Seat long engaged attention—Lists of plants at various dates—Many wild plants now disappearing from old stations—Plants at the castle, &c.—"A natural rock-garden"—Aquatic plants of Duddingston Loch—The "Craigmillar Sycamore"—Seedlings from the old tree—Seedling planted by Lord Rosebery at Linlithgow Palace—Inscription at foot of tree—List of some of the native plants 124

VI.—GEOLOGICAL FEATURES OF THE DISTRICT.

Few districts so interesting to the geologist—Various "systems" represented—The Carboniferous rocks—The Igneous rocks—Fossils of the district—Examples of glacial action—Craigmillar building-stone—Public and private buildings and other structures for which stone was used—"Hard labour" for female offenders—The Picts said to have built Edinburgh Castle from Craigmillar quarry 152

VII.—THE ENVIRONS OF CRAIGMILLAR.

Panorama from battlements of Craigmillar Castle—History of The Inch—Its successive proprietors—Cromwell's sword at The Inch House—Nether Liberton—The Boroughmoor and Blackford Hill

—The Barony of Over Liberton—Liberton Village—John Pounds and Dr Guthrie—Proprietors of Upper Liberton—Liberton House and its architectural features—Structural design of Liberton Tower—The Braid Hills—Mortonhall—The Balm Well—Burdiehouse and Straiton — The Pentlands — Rullion Green — The Martyrs' Monument — Hugh M'Kail — Old Woodhouselee— Hamilton of Bothwellhaugh and the Regent Murray—The modern Woodhouselee—The Tytler family—Relics of Queen Mary at Woodhouselee 168

VIII.—PROXIMATE LANDSCAPE.

Duddingston village and loch—Duddingston parish church—The Rev. Robert Monteith—The Rev. John Thomson—Easter Duddingston Lodge—Peffer Mill—"Half-hangit Maggie Dickson"— Craigmillar Irrigated Meadows—The ancient forest of Drumselch—Large antlers of red deer found—Bridgend—Priestfield or Prestonfield—Niddrie—The Wauchopes of Niddrie—Colonel Wauchope of the Black Watch—Edmonstone—Little France— Kingston Grange—Moredun—Story of Baron Moncrieff and James Boswell—Stenhouse—The Stenhouse witches—Lady Gilton—Hyvot's Mill—Gilmerton—The "subterranean cave"— The tragedy of Burntdool—The Drum—Successive proprietors of the Drum—CONCLUSION 206

INDEX 243

LIST OF ILLUSTRATIONS.

		PAGE
CRAIGMILLAR CASTLE,	*Frontispiece*	
CAPTAIN GORDON GILMOUR,	*To face*	52
A GROUP OF NEWTS,	,,	74
ARTHUR'S SEAT AND QUEEN'S PARK,	,,	126
THE INCH HOUSE,	,,	170
LIBERTON INDUSTRIAL SCHOOL PIPERS,	,,	182
WILLIAM CHARLES LITTLE OF LIBERTON,	,,	188
TOMBSTONE IN MEMORY OF THE COVENANTERS AT RULLION GREEN,		198
DUDDINGSTON LOCH,	,,	208
PEFFER MILL HOUSE,	,,	212
KINGSTON GRANGE,		226
GILMERTON SUBTERRANEAN CAVE,	,,	238
GROUND-PLAN OF CRAIGMILLAR CASTLE,		3
ORIGINAL ENTRANCE TO KEEP,		4
FIREPLACE IN GREAT HALL,		6
DOORWAY TO MAIN STAIRCASE,		14
SOUTH-EAST TOWER,		16
CORBELLED CHAMBER ON SOUTH SIDE,		17
THE CHAPEL,		20

List of Illustrations.

Sculptured Stones,	21, 22, 23
Edinburgh from Craigmillar,	24
Preston Arms, with Supporters,	28
View from Craigmillar, looking East,	30
Woolmet,	43
Sir John Gilmour, President of Court of Session,	45
The Gilmour Crest,	53
The Badger,	55
Long-eared and Daubenton's Bats,	63
Voles,	68
Long-tailed Duck,	82
The Quail,	84
The Pet Kingfisher,	85
The Barn Owl,	86
Cuckoo fed by a Wagtail,	90
"Jacky," the Liberton Magpie,	95
The Great Spotted Woodpecker,	99
The Goatsucker or Night-jar,	104
The Swift,	115
Chaffinch, Bullfinch, and Crossbill,	121
Queen Mary's Tree,	139
Scale of Fish (*Rhizodus Hibbertii*),	159
Portion of Jaw of Fish (*Rhizodus Hibbertii*),	160
Ice-worn Surface of Rock, Queen's Drive,	162
Carboniferous Fern (*Sphenopteris affinis*),	167
The Inch House as it was,	169
Cromwell's Sword, at The Inch House,	172
Old Cottages at The Inch,	174

List of Illustrations.

Dovecot and Mill-dam, Nether Liberton,	175
"Good's Corner," Nether Liberton,	176
Liberton, from the Boroughmoor,	179
Liberton Industrial School,	180
Peep of Liberton House,	187
Liberton Tower,	190
View from the Braids,	192
Mortonhall,	194
Solitaire, worn by Queen Mary,	204
Queen Mary's Watch, at Woodhouselee,	205
Entrance Door, Peffer Mill,	211
Dormer Window and Sun-dial, Peffer Mill,	212
Bridgend, from the Suburban Railway,	214
Prestonfield, from Arthur's Seat,	216
Niddrie House,	218
Edmonstone House, from Craigmillar Woods,	223
Moredun House,	227
View in Moredun Park,	229
Stenhouse,	232
Hyvot's Mill,	233
Gilmerton House,	235
Gilmerton, looking East,	236
Drum House,	240
Drum House, from the South-East,	241

Craigmillar and its Environs.

I.

The Castle—Its Architectural Features.

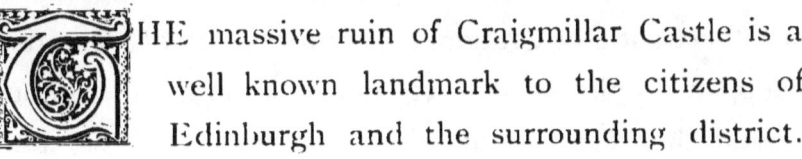HE massive ruin of Craigmillar Castle is a well known landmark to the citizens of Edinburgh and the surrounding district. It is also an object of attraction to strangers visiting Edinburgh from all parts of the world, by reason of the associations and traditions with which its history is invested. From its battlements a magnificent panoramic scene meets the gaze of the observer. To the north towers venerable Arthur's Seat, beneath whose shadow Duddingston Church and Loch lie calm and peaceful. A little to the west, the metropolis, with its castle and numerous spires, stands out in bold relief. In the distance is the Firth of Forth, ever widening towards the ocean, with the Bass Rock and North

Berwick Law conspicuously prominent. Behind are Liberton Kirk and parish, Gilmerton, Straiton, and various other villages; the whole being bounded by the Pentland, Moorfoot, and Lammermoor ranges.

The Castle of Craigmillar comprises an old Scottish keep, in style similar to many others throughout Scotland. It was of old a famous fortress, and belonged in time of war to the king, no subject being allowed to build castles or strongholds on any other condition. Extensive additions have been made to the castle from time to time. The keep, occupying the centre of the south front, stands on the edge of a cliff about twenty feet high, and is so near the edge that there is scanty room left for access to the door; while at some parts a foothold at the top of the rocks is all that can be obtained. Immediately in front of the door a deep indentation in the rock almost intersects the path, and before the additions to the castle changed the aspect of affairs, this cutting must have made it almost impregnable, as, apart from the door, there was no other opening on the ground floor except one small window a few inches

The Castle—Its Architectural Features.

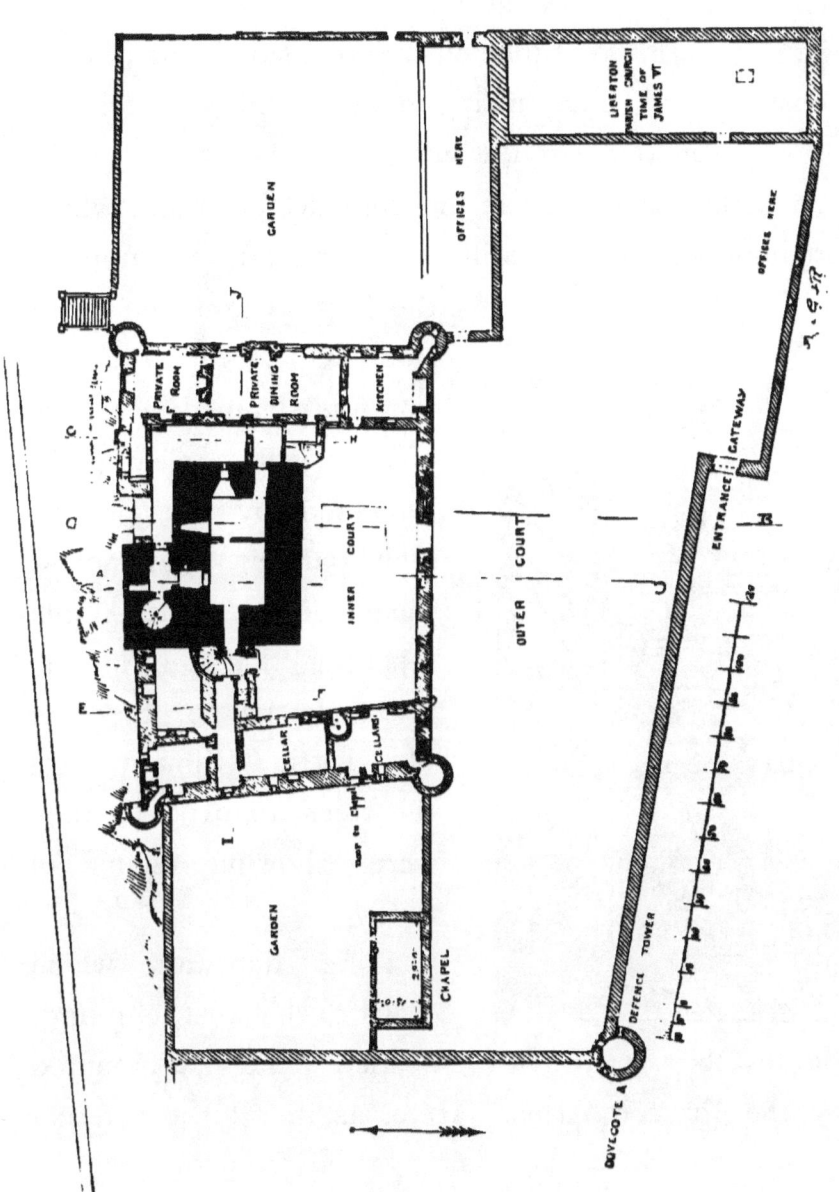

Ground-plan of the Castle.

wide, the other entrance on the west side being of later construction. The cutting in the rock is now bridged over by a modern arch, which carries the footpath leading to the doorway, but the difficulty of access which originally existed will still be understood by examining the fortress from the south side. Up to 1884 this cutting was spanned by trunks of trees, and a clear path, protected by the present high parapet, laid across the dangerous point. While repairing the ruin in the year referred to, the late Mr Little Gilmour had the trees removed, as they were showing signs of decay.

ORIGINAL ENTRANCE TO KEEP.

The doorway, which looks to the west, is round-headed, and surmounted by the Preston Arms. Here, as in all the external entrances to the Castle, are to be seen long holes cut in the walls, to receive sliding beams, by which the doors were barricaded across. About nine feet from the door the passage divides, the branch on the left hand leading to the ground floor, and the one in front to the staircase. By the former the visitor enters a small chamber, limited in its dimensions by the thickness of the wall, and from which he passes into the large chamber on the ground floor. This is vaulted by a lofty arch, beneath which there was an intermediate floor of wood. The under floor was divided by a partition wall into two apartments. The upper chamber, evidently reached by a ladder, was lighted by a window at each end, and had a door of communication with the small chamber above referred to.

The staircase leading to the Great Hall has a peculiar arrangement. It is a corkscrew stair, and after ascending about ten feet by a couple of revolutions, it suddenly comes to a stop, when, turning abruptly to the left, another staircase begins, by which the ascent is completed. If the first stair had been continued upwards, it would have landed in the room known as "Queen Mary's Room." At the beginning of the second staircase a doorway overlooks the entrance hall, and the shifting of the staircase here to the side has evidently been for the purpose of securing more space

FIREPLACE IN GREAT HALL.

for the action of men defending the castle. In the event of the outer door being forced, an enemy could from this point be most severely handled by the inmates, with comparative immunity from danger.

The Great Hall is a noble apartment, 35 feet

long, 20 feet 9 inches wide, and 20 feet 6 inches high, to the apex of its arched roof. The walls, which are of an average thickness of 9 feet, are pierced by windows on the north, south, and east, all provided with stone seats. These are each large enough to accommodate six or seven persons, and would be useful as retiring places. The fireplace is a fine specimen of its kind, and is well preserved. There was a crack in the lintel, but the late proprietor, Mr Little Gilmour, had it secured by an iron band. Beside it a doorway leads down by steps to the more modern part of the castle on the west. The hall has been divided into two storeys. The stone corbels for supporting the central beams are painted, the ornaments on them being still distinct, but of the painting on the vault above very little remains. Off the hall there is, as already indicated, a small arched room, known as "Queen Mary's Room." It is partly furnished, having a table and a few chairs which are used nowadays by picnic parties. There is also an old flint gun and a coat of mail, which tradition asserts to have belonged to Darnley. On the wall is a print of Queen Mary, with the following beautiful verses by Mr Scott Riddell subjoined:—

> "Yes, thou art Mary, Scotland's Queen,
>   Embodied forth by magic art,
> An image that long, long hath been
>   Enshrined within a nation's heart:
> And who can gaze upon thee now,
>   And know no sorrow for the tears
> Wrung from thy heart in passing through
>   The pilgrimage of hapless years?
>
> We feel there is a mournful charm,
>   That hides thy frailties in decay,
> While thinking how a heart so warm
>   Could e'er grow cold as other clay.
> The white rose shall no sweets impart,
>   The thistle wave no longer green,
> Ere time shall melt from Scotland's heart
>   The memory of her lovely Queen."

As is usual in castles of this type, the stair leading to the top is not a continuation of the lower one. On the opposite side of the passage leading into the Great Hall another spiral staircase ascends. At the first landing a door leads into the floor already referred to as having existed over the hall, and another to an entresol room over "Queen Mary's Room." This latter is a very beautiful apartment, of plain and simple architecture. Adjoining it is a most complete garde-robe. Continuing up the staircase, the top is reached, where steps branch off on either side, leading, the one to the roof and the other to the upper and now roofless room over Queen Mary's. The introduction of this room seems to be a change on the original design. On the south front and at the floor level are two corbels, probably the remains of machicolations continued round the three faces of this projecting part of the castle, while the main flat roof was in all likelihood continued over this part. It is not easy otherwise to account for the corbels referred to. There is further a decided change in the masonry at this level, the stones being smaller and the windows larger in proportion to the size of the room. The rybats, too, are wrought with rounded edges instead of splays, as elsewhere throughout the keep. Doing away with the machicolations, leaving two of the corbels, heightening the wall plumb with the face below, putting on a high pitched roof, and thus gaining a room, are other results of the change.

The main roof is very flat, and was originally covered with overlapping stones, the under stone being wrought with a groove along the sides of its upper surface. Two rows thus wrought were laid in their sloping position, with a space between for the overlapping stones, which extended over the grooves, the object of this being that rain blown in beneath the edges of the overlapping row would be caught in the groove, and thus run down to the carefully formed gutter. Prior to 1884 the roof was in a very dilapidated condition, in consequence of rain and snow getting in, the stones of some of the fine arches were being dislodged by frost, and it was very apparent that unless steps were taken to preserve the ruin, it would soon become a shadowy relic of the past.

In the spring of the year referred to, the Edinburgh Architectural Association paid a visit to Craigmillar, and reported the matter to Mr Little Gilmour. With great public spirit, and at very considerable expense, that gentleman had extensive repairs carried out on the building, care being taken that no damp should get down through the masonry. As only a part of the overlapping stones of the roof could be found, these were put in on the south-west corner, and the remainder of the roof was carefully made watertight with cement.

The parapet round the roof is brought up flush with the face of the walls, and most of the embrasures can still be traced. The roof was doubtless constructed flat for the convenience of working military engines. The total height of the keep from the top of the rock is about seventy feet, and to the base about ninety feet. The additions which have been made at various times have considerably altered the aspect and internal arrangements of the castle, especially with regard to the entrance. In the first instance, a great curtain wall was erected, the keep itself forming a part on the south, with angle towers, and enclosing a courtyard. The space within the outer walls averages 122 feet from east to west by 80 feet from north to south. Later, and at various times, within this courtyard, buildings have been added against the curtain walls on the east, west, and south sides. The entrance gateway was in the north curtain.

Beyond this to the east, west, and north are outer walls, strong and high, enclosing a space of about 1¼ acre within the castle bounds, which formed the outer bailey or courtyard. The south wall is merely a continuation of the castle front along the top of the precipice. Within these walls, again, various offices were built at different times. The outer wall on the north side runs nearly parallel with the north curtain, and a little beyond the line of the curtain door it turns off at right angles outwards for about 17 feet, and in this space is contained the first or outer entrance, being a round arched gateway, 7 feet 4 inches wide by 10 feet 6 inches high, in a wall 4 feet 6 inches thick. The position of this gateway is so chosen that, in the event of its being forced, the assailants would not be able to make a straight rush to the door in the curtain wall. It is also commanded by a round tower at the north-east corner, which guards the east wall likewise. This tower was also fitted up as a pigeon-house.

The curtain walls are about 28 feet high to the top of the parapet, and 5 feet thick. In the north wall, but not in the centre, is situated the doorway, and inside on either hand is an arched recess about 9 feet above the ground, having a spy window and stone seat for a sentinel. These were reached by ladders from enclosed recesses beneath.

The east range of buildings is three storeys high, the first two storeys being vaulted. A gloomy sunk floor at the south end is reached by a separate stair, off which runs a lobby leading to the bakery, which has a very complete well-constructed oven. Adjoining the bakery is the well room, and on the opposite side of the passage is a low, dark dungeon, with a private trap-stair to the room above, and a narrow drain through the wall, having a kind of sink at both ends. A human skeleton was discovered here in 1813 by John Pinkerton, Advocate, and Mr Irvine, W.S., but on being exposed to the air it shortly crumbled into dust. From the fact of its being found in an upright position, Sir Walter Scott and others who visited the place were of opinion that the victim had been immured alive.

It has been asserted that from the dungeon a

subterranean passage at one time communicated with the mansion-house of Peffer Mill. This tradition, however, is not borne out by facts. A layer of Craigmillar rock runs through the entire intervening ground, and from its adamantine nature the cutting of a subterranean passage was highly improbable. The matter was, however, set at rest when the Suburban Railway was constructed, excavations being made through the line of the supposed tunnel at a very considerable depth, when no trace whatever of a subterranean passage was discovered.

DOORWAY TO MAIN STAIRCASE.

The beautiful doorway in the east range of buildings erected about the time of Queen Mary, became the principal entrance to the keep, in place of the old doorway in the south-west side. From the doorway a wide spiral staircase led up to the Great Hall and upper floors of the new wing.

On the ground floor of the east wing are offices and a large room, to the south. A private stair in the south-east corner led down to a postern in the west side of this tower, which was doubtless found to be a dangerous convenience, and it was ultimately built up, the steps being removed, the tower made into a closet, and the large room divided by a thick partition. At the side of the east doorway above referred to, and in the thickness of the wall, a separate stair leads up to the kitchen, which has a large arched fireplace, a stone sink with drain, and a service window into the corridor leading to the Great Hall. The room adjoining the kitchen to the north was a private apartment, having a separate staircase from the courtyard. From the floor above the kitchen the east and north battlements are reached through the south-east tower. These are supported on bold corbels with machicolations, through which stones could be thrown on an enemy approaching the base of the walls. The corbels of the corner towers are slightly higher than those of the walls, and somewhat different in construction, owing to their smaller projection. The upright parts of the battlements are splayed away over the openings, so as to increase the range of the defenders' missiles.

Prior to 1884 there was a large mass of earth on the roof of the north-east tower. This was doubtless placed there for the purpose of minimising the destructive effect of stones thrown from mangonels or catapults. Below six feet of this earth a large stone, with the Preston Arms and supporters, carefully laid face downwards, was discovered, and was built into the wall above the doorway to the main staircase. In the centre of the south-east tower is a raised platform, reached by steps, from which shots could be fired over the

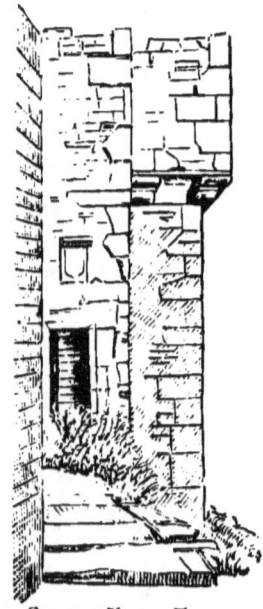
SOUTH-EAST TOWER.

heads of those defending the battlements. A narrow stair in this tower leads to the battlement of the south front. Projected on comparatively small corbels, it stretches towards the keep for about thirty-three feet, and although at a lower level than the battlements just described, it is, on account of the precipice, higher above the ground. The parapet has disappeared, but it was of more than ordinary height between the embrasures. At the keep end of the balcony is a small apartment formed by a bold, massive, projecting structure leading from the room inside.

When the west wing came to be added, the west curtain was nearly all taken down, and rebuilt as it now stands, with windows and chimneys, and without the machicolations. This was the latest addition made to the castle. The west wing is two storeys high, with vaults at the south end. Although built in a lighter style than any other part,

CORBELLED CHAMBER ON SOUTH SIDE.

it still gives evidence of a desire on the part of its owners for security, and their determination that there should be no entrance to the garden, which is on this side, except by the roundabout way through the north curtain. The rooms in this wing are large and handsome, entering through each other in the style of the seventeenth century. This was evidently the residential part, with its separate entrance from the courtyard, kitchen, dining-room, and private bedrooms. The dining-room had a beautiful fireplace, lined with Dutch tiles, and a window with a mullion and transom. Off a short court at the south end, and also communicating with the rooms, is a small retiring room with a garde-robe projecting outside, and window with seats. It is probably owing to the quatrefoil light in this room, giving it an ecclesiastical look, that it has been called the "Confessional" in some local guide-books. Communication with other parts of the castle was by a stair between the west wing and the keep, and through the Great Hall on to the rooms beyond. The bowling-green was on the west side, immediately outside of this range of buildings, and from it a flight of steps led down to the gardens at the lower level. Here the bed of the fish-pond can still be seen in the shape of the letter "P," no doubt intended for "Preston." The steps are now quite ruinous, and the dies serve for gate pillars at the entrance to the neighbouring farm-house. The present proprietor, Captain Gordon Gilmour, who takes a great interest in the ruin, intends having these restored to their original position. . When the additions referred to were made to the castle, the old south curtain wall was not taken down, and as it now stands is most interesting, exhibiting a complete arrangement for the erection of a bretêche or hoarding for defence. A row of corbels runs along the curtain, and above them the holes for the projecting putlogs for supporting the hoarding, and a wooden gallery which enabled the defenders to see the foot of the wall, and to throw stones or other missiles upon assailants. A row of upper corbels, carefully checked on top for the beam supporting the roof of the hoarding, is still in position, while the door leading out to it from the level of the upper floor also exists, now built up and forming a press inside. An iron ring, still existing at the side of this door, was probably meant for the rope or chain used to fix up the trap-door in the floor of the hoarding.

Between the east curtain and the outside wall is a small chapel, roofless, but otherwise entire, measuring

THE CHAPEL.

inside about 30 feet by 14 feet 9 inches. The door is at the west end of the south front. The chapel has been lighted by two square-headed windows on the south side, the eastern one having a mullion, and a small circular window high up in the west gable. Inside there is a carved piscina. Except that the

The Castle—Its Architectural Features.

gables have crow-steps, the chapel is very similar in style to the work of the Perpendicular period in England. The large, ivy-covered building at the west end was, as stated by the Rev. Thomas White, minister of Liberton, who wrote about 1752, "a Protestant Presbyterian meeting-house," erected upon an indulgence granted by James VII. of Scotland.[1] It was probably at first one of the barns or offices connected with the castle, and turned to this purpose. Above the doorway are the Preston Arms, with the date 1549.

All writers on Craigmillar, including the Rev. Thomas White, Sir Walter Scott, and Dr John Hill Burton, refer to the arms of the Cockburns, Congaltons, Mowbrays, and Otterburns, as adorning the walls of the castle. None of these, however, are here now, nor any other except the Preston Arms, which occur four times, and the Royal Arms, which surmount the Preston Arms over the entrance above the north gateway into inner courtyard, and again over the door leading to the south battlements

REBUS.

[1] Transactions of the Antiquarian Society.

at the east end. Besides these there is a rebus on the name "Pres-tun," and on the parapets of the east and north curtain are holes which form the centre of letters—those to the north being the letters "P" for Preston and "G" probably for Gorton, the family being sometimes styled "of Craigmillar," sometimes "of Gourton."[1] The letter on the east parapet may be either a "P" or an "R." In a large stone built into this curtain the letter "S" is pierced. It evidently stands for Symon Preston, the well known Provost of Edinburgh, and friend of Queen Mary. On the outside of the north curtain is a large projecting stone basin about five feet above the ground, and having a stone pipe led through the wall into the north-east corner of the courtyard for passing in a supplementary water supply to the castle.

SHOT HOLES IN PARAPET.

SHOT HOLES IN PARAPET.

We gather from these records of bygone days a lesson not merely instructive to the antiquarian,

---

[1] Gorton stands on the South Esk, Mid-Lothian.

but to all thoughtful students of history and of human nature. We here learn that even the greatest nobles of the land are amenable to those elements of change which decree that no family, however noble and formidable in social and political influence, can retain a permanent monopoly in the possessions of a fickle and fleeting world.

PRESTON ARMS OVER ENTRANCE.

II.

Craigmillar Castle—Its Historical Associations.

THE name of Craigmillar is said to be derived from the Gaelic *craig-moil-ard*, signifying a high and bare rock, which no doubt accurately described the site prior to the erection of the castle. Variations in the name

EDINBURGH FROM CRAIGMILLAR.

have occurred, as usual in such matters, from time to time. Thus we find it referred to in ancient documents as Cragmillar, Craigmillare, Cragmeloure, Cragmelor, and Cragmulor. As to when or by whom the castle was built history is, however, silent.[1] The earliest record of Craigmillar is in 1137, when David I. gave to the Holy Trinity Church of Dunfermline, in perpetual gift, some houses in Craigmillar, with several acres of arable land. The next authentic notice of Craigmillar is in 1212, and is found in a charter of mortification granted in the reign of Alexander II. by William, son of Henricus de Craigmillar. In this charter William gives "in pure and perpetual alms, to the church and monastery of Dunfermline, a certain toft of land in Craigmillar, in the southern part thereof, which leads from the town of Nedrieff [Niddry] to the church of Libberton, which Henricus de Edmonstone holds of him."[2] Craigmillar after-

---

[1] In 'Castellated Architecture of Scotland' Messrs M'Gibbon and Ross give their opinion that Craigmillar must have been built in the fourteenth century.

[2] See 'Historical and Statistical Account of the Town and Parish of Dunfermline,' by the Rev. Dr Chalmers, vol. ii. pp. 228, 229.

wards became the property of John de Capella, of whom little is known; and from his family it passed in 1374 to that of the Prestons of Gorton, who were an important family in Scotland at that time—Sir Symon Preston having obtained from King Robert II. a charter of the lands of "Cragmelor," in the county of Edinburgh, on the resignation of William de Capella. The Prestons were possessors of Craigmillar for a period of 300 years. Their name is derived from the barony of Prestoun or Priest's town, now Gorton, on the South Esk, Mid-Lothian. It may be of interest to mention that Sir William de Preston, Knight, was one of the barons of Scotland summoned to Norham Castle by King Edward I., in the competition for the crown betwixt Baliol and Bruce in 1291. On this occasion a large number of the nobility and clergy assembled to decide the question, on the Scottish side of the Tweed, upon a large open plain called Upsettlington, now included in the beautiful wooded policies of Ladykirk. Mr David Beveridge, in his 'Culross and Tulliallan,' states that Sir John de Preston, Knight, was taken prisoner with David II.

at the Battle of Durham in 1346, and was confined for a long time in the Tower of London. Sir John obtained from David II. charters of the lands of Gorton, and also of lands in Fife and Perthshire. His son was the Symon de Preston already referred to. Though there is some doubt as to who really were Sir Symon's children, there is every reason to believe that he was the father of George de Preston, who, again, was the father of John Preston of Craigmillar and Gorton, from whom the Prestons of Craigmillar were descended. The Prestons of Valleyfield sprang from the same family, though the precise period at which they branched off is a matter of some dispute. As already mentioned, the Preston Arms—a shield bearing the heads of three unicorns—are found four times on the walls of Craigmillar. The same emblem appears in St Giles' Cathedral, William Preston being recognised as a benefactor of that church. In the reign of James II. this William Preston seems to have gone to France, and, with the aid of King Charles VII. and other magnates, to have obtained a precious relic—the arm-bone of St Giles.

Returning to Scotland, he soon afterwards died, bequeathing the celebrated relic to the Church of Edinburgh; and he was buried in the Lady Chapel of St Giles'. The gift of Preston was received by the

PRESTON ARMS, WITH SUPPORTERS.

city with all due honour, and the Town Council came under an obligation to his son to build the aisle to his memory which still bears his name, and on which his arms are engraved.

On August 10, 1511, James IV. conceded to Simon

Preston of Preston, Knight, and to his heirs, "the lands of Cragmelor, with their castle, fortalice, and mill, and the patronage and donation of the chapel founded in the lands of Cameron"; and the King incorporated all the same in the free barony of Craigmillar. Again, on June 5, 1543, the Queen conceded to Simon Preston, son and heir-apparent of George Preston, and Janet, his spouse, the lands and barony of Cragmelor, with castle, fortalice, and mill. Sir Simon Preston was, on August 15, 1565, on the representation of Queen Mary, made Lord Provost of Edinburgh, but he afterwards broke away from his allegiance, and it was in his house that the Queen was lodged the night before she was carried to Lochleven. In Fountainhall's 'Historical Notices' (p. 189) it is stated that on May 2, 1678, John Preston was excluded by the Duke of Lauderdale from commission, as one inclined to burn too many as witches. We learn on the same authority (p. 200) that John Preston, along with other three, were on commission to judge seven who were defamed as witches in Loanhead.

Reverting to Craigmillar, it is perhaps worthy of

note that the barony is held of the Crown in free blench for payment of two pennies Scots—*i.e.*, 2-12ths of a penny sterling—at Whitsunday yearly, at the tower, fortalice, and manor place of Craigmillar, in name of blench duty—if asked only. There is no

VIEW FROM CRAIGMILLAR—LOOKING EAST.

reservation as to the giving up of the castle for a royal residence, as has been asserted by some writers. That it possesses all the natural features associated with a royal residence is indisputable. Few sites in any part of Scotland have such a commanding range of country, alike diversified and picturesque. Looking in a southern and western direction, there is a view of strath, gently sloping valley, and woodland, which roll on until backed by high mountain ranges far beyond. Towards the north, the fertile fields of Fifeshire meet the eye, the "East Neuk" stretching away into the German Ocean in the distance. Looking eastward, there opens up such a charming prospect of land and water, that the eye of the beholder never wearies in gazing upon it. There is the blue gleaming ocean, which washes the shore only a few miles from the ancient castle, and stretches far away in the distance, leaving North Berwick Law and the Bass Rock as impressive landmarks; while Aberlady Bay, fringed with the green woodlands of Gosford, fill up the picture. Such a landscape, viewed from Craigmillar Castle on a beautiful spring morning, or a still summer's eve, by the lover of nature, is one upon which memory delights to dwell.

In 1477 Craigmillar was the scene of a curious state tragedy. The Duke of Albany and the Earl of Mar having been charged with conspiracy against their brother, James III., the Duke was apprehended and lodged in the Castle of Edinburgh, but he managed to escape to a sloop which waited for him in the Forth to take him to France. The Earl of Mar, however, was less fortunate, and was imprisoned in Craigmillar. Unlike King James, Albany and Mar were active and warlike, displaying much of the chivalrous spirit of their ancestors, and thus they became endeared to the people. Pitscottie, in his description of their different characters, says of James that he was "a man that loved solitariness, and desired never to hear of warre." On the other hand, Mar, he says, was "ain faire lustie man of ain great and weill proportioned stature, weill faced, and comillie in his behaviour, who was nothing but nobilitie." Whether it was really a fact that the conspiracy against the King was contemplated, or whether it was only an idle report got up to frighten James, and make him suspicious and jealous of his brother, is uncertain. Some writers affirm that Mar was privately beheaded, while others assert that he was asked to choose his own mode of death, which he did by preferring to be bled in a warm bath. On the other hand, Drummond of Hawthornden states—and he is supported by Tytler—that Mar, who was very excitable, took fever and delirium, and was removed by command of the King to a house in the Canongate. There he was put under the care of the King's physician, who relieved him in his fever by opening a vein in the arm and neck. Whether from weakness consequent on the loss of blood, or from tearing his bandages off while in a fit of delirium, does not seem clear, but Mar did not survive this attack. The actual circumstances are to a great extent shrouded in mystery. Dr John Hill Burton, in his excellent 'History of Scotland,' says: "We know only the fact that the King dealt with both his brothers as a man deals with his enemies. The younger, Mar, died suddenly—murdered, it was said—in Craigmillar Castle. Those who desired to vindicate the King's name said Mar had been bled to relieve him from fever, and that the bleeding, being insufficiently stanched, had broken out while he was in a bath, and so killed him."

That Craigmillar ever became a royal residence,

there is not sufficient authority to affirm positively. James V., however, being kept a prisoner in Edinburgh Castle during his minority, was removed to Craigmillar in 1514, when the plague broke out in the city, to be out of the way of infection. While there, he was privileged to see his mother under certain restrictions, through the kindness of his guardian, Lord Erskine.

Craigmillar was taken by the English invaders under Hertford, and was partly demolished, a great part of it being burned. John Knox, in his 'History of the Reformation,' describing the entry of the English army under the Earl of Hertford into Leith in 1544, says: "Upon the Mononday the fyft of May, came to thame from Berwick and the Bordour two thousand horsemen, who, being somewhat reposed, the army, upoun the Wednesday, marched towards the Toune of Edinburgh, spoyled and brynt the same, and so did thei the Palace of Halirud-house. The horsmen took the House of Craigmyllare, and gat great spoyle therein; for it being judged the strongest house near the Toune, other than the Castell of Edinburgh, all men sought to saif thare movables tharein.

But the stoutness of the Lorde gave it over without schote of hacque-boote, and for his reward was caused to march upoun his foote to Londoun. He is now Capitane of Dunbar, and Provost of Edinburgh.

In the 'Diurnal of Occurrents' we read: "The English forces passed to Craigmillar, quhilk was haistilie given to thame; promesed to keip the samyne without skaith, quhilk promes thai brak, and brunt and destroyit the said Hous."

It is, however, in the time of the young and beautiful though unfortunate Mary Stuart that much of the interest in Craigmillar centres. The presumption is that it was chosen by her as a residence on account of its delightful surroundings; and being but a short distance from the Palace, she could easily travel between the two places. The ground, too, was admirably adapted for hunting, in which pastime Darnley and the members of the royal household could indulge.

Shortly after the murder of Rizzio in 1566, on account of which Darnley and Mary became much estranged, the whole kingdom was curious to ascertain what would be the next turn of events. We find the

French Ambassador at the court of Holyrood, Le Croc, writing to the Archbishop of Glasgow in December of that year in the following terms: " The Queen is for the present at Craigmillar, about a league distant from the city. She is in the hands of the physicians, and I do assure you is not at all well; and I do believe the principal part of her disease to consist of a deep grief and sorrow—nor does it seem possible to make her forget the same. Still she repeats these words, ' I could wish to be dead.' We know very well that the injury she received is exceeding great, and her Majesty will never forget it. . . . To speak my mind freely to you—but I beg you not to disclose what I say in any place that may turn to my prejudice—I do not expect upon several accounts any good understanding between them, unless God effectually put to His hand." In the same year Craigmillar was the scene of a conference between Queen Mary and her nobles regarding a proposed divorce from Darnley, but this proposal for the time was overruled by her. The conference was attended by Lethington, Argyll, and Bothwell. The first-named was the spokesman on that occasion, and the result is thus given in the words of those who initiated the business: "Her grace answerit, that under twa conditions she might understand the same—the ane, that the divorcement were made lawfully; the other, that it war not prejudice to her son—otherwise her hyness would rather endure all torments, and abyde the perils that might chance her in her grace's lifetime." In Pitcairn's 'Criminal Trials' it is stated that four of those then present—viz., Argyll, Huntly, Maitland, and Bothwell—along with a cousin of the last, Sir James Balfour, signed a bond to the following effect: "That forsaemickle it was thought expedient and maist profitable for the commonwealth, by the haill nobility and lords under subscryvit, that sic ane young fool and proud tyrant suld not reign or bear rule over them; and that for divers causes, therefore, they had all concluded that he suld be put off by ane way or another—and whosoever suld take the deed in hand, or do it, they suld defend and fortify it as themselves."[1] It was by the merest

[1] This passage from the bond was cited from memory by the Laird of Ormiston, in his confession. See *post*, p. 39.

chance that the walls of Craigmillar escaped being stained with the blood of Darnley. In 1567, when he returned from Glasgow ill with smallpox, before determining to send him to the Kirk-of-Field, as was afterwards done in order to keep infection from the infant prince at Holyrood, a proposal was mooted to lodge him in Craigmillar, that he might have there the benefit of the pure air and the warm bath, and so have a speedy recovery. In the eyes of Darnley and his friends, as well as of others, this seemed an ominous proposal, considering what had befallen Mar in former days. The Queen seems to have made the suggestion; and as soon as it had been proposed to Darnley, he sent for Craufurd, and, relating the circumstances, requested that the whole should be communicated to his father, the Earl of Lennox. Craufurd, being asked his own opinion on the proposal, said: "She treats your Majestie too like a prisoner. Why should you not be taken to one of your own houses in Edinburgh?" "It struck me much the same," said Darnley. "Between us, I have her promise only to trust to; but I put myself in her hands, and I will go with her though she murder me." Whether Mary was cognisant of any plot to get rid of her husband, or whether she simply advised him for his good, is still a matter on which much diversity of opinion exists.

Bothwell, generally regarded as chief actor in the plot, followed the Queen to Craigmillar after the murder, and a few months later Mary accepted him as her husband. From this fact many have concluded that the Queen could not have been altogether ignorant of the dark deed consummated at Kirk-of-Field. On the other hand, it is recorded that the Laird of Ormiston, who was convicted upwards of six years after the murder of Darnley, made a confession to the Rev. John Brand, during his last moments, while the latter was trying to cheer him with the consolations of religion. In this confession, already referred to, he stated that Bothwell spoke to him on the subject of the murder only two days before it was committed, and that "he utterly refused to join the plot." Bothwell also informed him that the bond had been drawn up by Sir James Balfour, and signed a quarter of a year before the deed was done. After the murder, Ormiston said, Bothwell showed him a bond signed by four or five names, which he assured him were those of Huntly, Argyll, Maitland, and Sir James Balfour. In Birrel's 'Diary' (p. 14) we learn that "on 3d Jan. 1568, John Hay of Talla, zounger, and John Hepburne of Bollone, and ane Powrie, and ane Dalgleish, seruitors to ye Earl of Bothwell, ver hangit and quartred, and their bodies brunt for murther of ye King." The Regent Morton was in June 1581 also tried and executed for the murder of Darnley, fourteen years after the event. Little is known of his trial, but he was found guilty of being "art and part, foreknowledge and concealing of the treasonable and unnatural murder" of the King. The principal evidence produced was the testament of Bothwell, who had died in Denmark in 1578. It is therefore assumed that this deed contained matter implicating Morton. We learn further from Pitcairn's 'Criminal Trials' that John Binning, a servant of Archibald Douglas, was also tried and convicted. Before his death Binning not only confessed that his master was concerned in the plot, but he also accused John Maitland, Abbot of Coldingham, brother of the Secretary, and Robert Balfour, brother of Sir James, and owner of the house at the Kirk-of-Field. For several years after the murder of Darnley no one was publicly charged with the murder, except Bothwell and the Queen. In course of time, however, when the nobles began to quarrel among themselves, Regent Morton, Archibald Douglas, Sir James Balfour—who was afterwards President of the Court of Session—Maitland the Secretary, Huntly the Chancellor, Argyll the Lord Justice, and a number of others, were all charged as being prominent actors in the tragedy; but nothing was ever discovered which could incriminate Queen Mary. Who the real culprits were it will perhaps be impossible ever to say with certainty.

Returning once more to Craigmillar Castle, James VI. was the last royal personage who lived in or was connected with it. From there he planned his matrimonial tour to Denmark. In the declaration, written by himself, of his reasons for his resolution to go to Norway, and of his own sole and entire responsibility for that resolution, with his narrative of what passed thereupon between him and his Councillors, he says: "The place that I resolved this in was Craigmillaire, no ain of the haill counsale being present there."[1]

After repeated insurrections of that turbulent nobleman Francis Stewart, second Earl of Bothwell, in the reign of James VI., a battle was fought near Craigmillar. On the 3d of April 1594, Bothwell and Lord Ochiltree marched to Leith, accompanied by four hundred valiant horsemen. The few noblemen and gentlemen that were in Edinburgh, along with the inhabitants of the town, armed themselves to assist the King, and marched in order of battle towards Leith. Bothwell, however, retreated by Restalrig to Duddingston, so that it appeared as if his intention was to flee. He continued retreating by Niddrie Marischall up the hill towards Woolmet. Thinking he had fled altogether, the King commanded Lord Home, the Master of Glammis, with their forces, and the guard of horsemen and footmen, to follow Bothwell. In accordance with these instructions, Bothwell was pursued to Niddrie Green, where a consultation was held before

[1] Register of the Privy Council of Scotland, vol. iv. p. 427.

the ascent to Woolmet. Here the forces were divided into two companies, the first of which, the King's Guard of Horsemen, was led by Lord Wemyss—"a gentilman of gude experience in werefayre." In the other company was Lord Home, the Master of

WOOLMET.

Glammis, and a number of gentlemen. Three horsemen were sent forward to reconnoitre before they thought it expedient to pass up. On the three getting near the top, Bothwell's ambuscade set upon them, and they were compelled to return as fast as their horses could carry them. Then Bothwell followed fiercely "with clamour and courage," so that within a short time he compelled his pursuers to leave their position and turn back. Bothwell continued the pursuit for over a mile, and chased them near to the place where the King and his company stood. The footmen fled for fear to the castle of Craigmillar. Bothwell's trumpet sounded a retreat "upon a fayre ley feild" under Craigmillar in sight of the King, and his host then retreated slowly back to Woolmet. Few were slain at the conflict, but a number were taken prisoners, and many hurt. The prisoners were set free by Bothwell the same night.[1]

Sir John Gilmour, son of John Gilmour, W.S., who was admitted a member of the Faculty of Advocates in 1628, acquired the property of the Barony of Craigmillar from the Prestons in 1660. He was four times married; and from his third wife, Margaret, eldest daughter of Sir Alexander Murray, Baronet of Blackbarony, in Peeblesshire, the present Captain Gilmour is descended. Sir John received knighthood in 1650,

[1] *Cf.* History of James the Sixth, p. 306.

SIR JOHN GILMOUR,
President of the Court of Session.
*From an Original Picture painted by old Scougal, at
The Inch, near Edinburgh.*

and was elected M.P. for Mid-Lothian to the Parliament that met 1st Jan. 1661, and to all the subsequent Parliaments until his death. In the year 1661 he was made President of the College of Justice, which office he resigned in 1670. Sir John was a thorough constitutionalist, and distinguished himself by opposing many of the arbitrary measures of his sovereign. Through his instrumentality a clause was obtained in the Militia Act, that the kingdom should not be obliged to maintain any force levied by the king without the consent of Parliament. Other memories reflect imperishable lustre on his name. When the Marquis of Argyll was brought to trial, Sir John argued with his brother judges that he could find no proof against him but what the greater part of the house were as deeply involved in as he was. The Earl of Middleton replied that what Sir John said was true, but that "the king may pitch upon whom he pleased to make an example of." As a privy councillor, Sir John refused to vote for the capital punishment of the Covenanters who had surrendered themselves on the promise of quarter after the battle of Rullion Green. He counselled mercy, but in vain, as Sharp, who presided at the council, was so much inflamed with rage that he overruled all the opposition and remonstrances of Sir John. Eleven prisoners constituted the first batch of victims. Little time was lost: they were quickly found guilty, and ordered to be hanged at the cross, and their heads and right arms to be cut off.

Sir John was said to be "most learned, though unassisted with the aid of the civil law; his own natural endowments made him equally conversant in the practice of the Scottish judicature as in that of the Romans; he might be said rather to lay down the law than to resolve questions in it; his clients consulted him rather as a judge than an advocate; he prostrated at his feet, as a second Hercules, the adverse parties with his knotted club, unsmoothed by any art; he was eloquent without rhetoric, learned without literature."[1]

Sir John altered and enlarged Craigmillar Castle considerably, and in Chambers's 'History of Peeblesshire' it is stated that "in 1661 the Council of

[1] Iconographia Scotica.

Peebles ordains that all able horses in the town shall carry in sklaitts from Stobo to the House of Craigmillar belonging to Sir John Gilmour, President of the Session; ilk person contravening under the pain of 5 pounds Scots." When it is taken into consideration that in those days there were no roads, and that the "sklaitts" had to be carried on the backs of horses a distance of thirty miles, this civic ordinance must appear a hard one, more especially when it was to serve one with whom the burgh had no concern. After a life of unvaried integrity and great usefulness, Sir John died in 1671, and his portrait is still carefully treasured in The Inch House. He was succeeded by his only surviving son, Sir Alexander Gilmour. Sir Alexander was created a Baronet on 1st February 1678; married the Hon. Grizel Ross, eldest daughter of George, eleventh Lord Ross,—his name is found in the Parliamentary records as one of the association to protect King William against the plot for his assassination by the papists,—and was elected M.P. for Mid-Lothian in 1698. Dying in October 1731, two children survived him—viz., Sir Charles Gilmour, his heir, and a daughter, Helen, who married William Little of Liberton. Sir Charles Gilmour, Baronet, married Jean Sinclair, daughter of Sir Robert Sinclair of Longformacus, was elected M.P. for Mid-Lothian in 1737, and continued to represent the county till his death. He was also one of the Lords of Trade and Plantations. He died at Montpellier in 1750, and left one child, Sir Alexander Gilmour, Baronet of Craigmillar, who was an officer in the 1st Foot Guards. Sir Alexander accompanied his regiment to France, and was taken prisoner at St Cas in September 1758. He was chosen M.P. for Mid-Lothian in 1751, and continued to represent that county till 1774. During that period he held various official appointments under Government. He died in France in 1792, and the Baronetcy and main line of the family thus became extinct. The succession then devolved on William Charles Little of Liberton, great-grandson of the first Sir Alexander Gilmour, and grandson of Sir Alexander's daughter, Helen Gilmour, who, as before mentioned, had been married to William Little of Liberton. Mr Little assumed in consequence the surname of Gilmour, and became also of Craigmillar. He married Jean Clerk, of the family of Pennycuick, and at his death in 1797 was succeeded by his eldest son, Walter Little Gilmour of Liberton and Craigmillar, who was an officer in the Army. Walter married in 1805 James Anne Macdowall, heiress of Canonmills, and died two years after, leaving a daughter, Jane, and a posthumous son, Walter James Little Gilmour. Mr Little Gilmour's education was begun at the Edinburgh High School and completed at Oxford. He was blest with a good mother, whose memory throughout life he never failed to cherish with feelings of almost sacred admiration. At an early age he manifested a great predilection for athletic exercises and field-sports, and at hunting, shooting, fishing, and golfing he was well known and honoured as a model sportsman. He was in his later years the oldest member of the Melton and Caledonian hunts, and was the last survivor of the group in the celebrated picture by the late Sir Francis Grant, President of the Royal Academy, the "Melton Breakfast." During his long career he was highly respected as a man of undoubted honour and integrity. His pleasing manners and amiable character earned for him the *sobriquet* of " Gentle," by which he was always addressed and spoken of by his friends. Though Mr Gilmour never resided on his property after the death of his mother, he always took a great interest in estate affairs, and especially in places of historic and public interest. In 1884, as already indicated, he, with great public spirit, spent a large sum for the purpose of preserving the ruins of Craigmillar Castle, which were rapidly going to decay. Repairs were in addition, though to a lesser extent, executed on the old Tower at Upper Liberton. Mr Gilmour was of a retiring disposition, and undemonstrative in his numerous acts of kindness and generosity, but few were ever more willing and ready to extend a helping hand to those who were really deserving, or to advance any enterprise which he was satisfied was for the public good. It may be here mentioned that Mr Gilmour was one of the " knights " present at the Eglinton tournament in 1839.

Mr Gilmour was never married, and when he died

in September 1887, the estates devolved upon Robert Wolrige Gordon, grandson of his sister Jane, already referred to.

Mr Wolrige Gordon is a son of Henry Wolrige Gordon of Hallhead and Esslemont, in Aberdeenshire, and assumed the name of Gilmour on succeeding to the Craigmillar property. He entered the army in January 1878, was made Lieutenant on 1st July 1881, and received a Captaincy on 23d July 1890. He served in the Zulu War in 1879, and took part in the engagements at Ulundi, for which he received the medal and clasp. He also served in the Nile expeditions in 1884-85 with the Guards Camel Regiment, and was present in the actions at Abu Klea and Abu Kru, for which he was honoured with a medal with two clasps and the Khedive's star. On 19th October 1889 Captain Gilmour married Lady Susan Lygon, second daughter of the late Earl Beauchamp of Madresfield Court, Worcestershire. Like his predecessor, he takes a great interest in the preservation of edifices of historic importance.

At what period Craigmillar was last tenanted does

Captain Gordon Gilmour.

not seem to be recorded, but Miss Warrender, in her admirable little book, 'Walks Near Edinburgh,' states that "till well into the eighteenth century two old ladies, daughters of Sir John Gilmour, lived there." It is stated elsewhere that at the close of the eighteenth century a part of the Castle was habitable, and occupied by a farmer.[1]

[1] See Grose's Antiquities of Scotland, vol. i. p. 51.

THE GILMOUR CREST.

III.

The Fauna.

THE representatives of our British fauna present in the environs of Craigmillar differ little from those found in most parts of the Lowlands of Scotland. It is gratifying to learn, however, that the BADGER, one of the scarcest of British wild creatures, is still to be seen within a mile of the castle ruins. We are inclined to think that this animal was for many years extinct in Mid-Lothian, and that through the accidental circumstance of a gravid female escaping from the kennels at The Inch, in the spring of 1883, they were again introduced to the district. So soon as it was discovered that badgers had been seen at Edmonstone, the proprietor, Sir John Don Wauchope, gave orders for their strict preservation.

Twice have they been known to breed there in recent years, and the thanks of all true naturalists are due to Sir John for his protective measures, despite the destruction caused by them to rabbits and other game. It is to be regretted, however, that these

THE BADGER.

animals still suffer persecution; and, though contrary to the proprietor's wishes, two were wantonly killed on the Edmonstone property in the spring of 1891.

OTTERS, though rare, are also to be found in the district. Twenty years ago they regularly frequented the policies of Duddingston; but in consequence of the rapid extension of Edinburgh to the south, the Braid Burn became polluted by the sewage, when trout disappeared, and along with them the otters. Some years since the town was interdicted from permitting sewage to pass into the brook, and a sewer was then built to convey it to the sea. From that time the brook has become practically pure, so that a few fish are now to be seen, and it is hoped that the otter may return to its former haunts. On the brook to the south of the castle which separates the Craigmillar property from that of Edmonstone, and which flows through the policies of Niddrie, otters have also been seen. A female otter and five cubs were observed from the drawing-room window of Niddrie House one summer evening, travelling up the side of the brook which flows close by. Securing pokers, some of the servants started on an otter hunt, and the water being shallow at the place, they succeeded in killing three of the cubs, which are to be seen, stuffed, in Niddrie House.

The Fox is frequently found in the district, and

so long as fox-hunting is regarded as a popular pastime, there is little fear of this animal becoming extinct. Fifty years ago Craigmillar was a favourite "meet" of the Duke of Buccleuch's hounds. The following account of a "run" was described to us by Sir John Don Wauchope, who was present. The hounds were advertised to meet at Craigmillar, and a fine morning brought out a large "field." Riding southwards, the hounds were thrown into the meadow between the Little France brooks, which at that time was an osier-bed, and a sure find for a fox. Reynard broke to the north, followed by a large number of the pack, and ran up the field in full view of every one present. Entering the wood east of the castle, which at that time contained a strong growth of whin and broom, constituting excellent cover, the fox lodged for a considerable time. The remainder of the pack getting up, the wood was made too hot for Reynard, and again he broke, running north by Duddingston, the hounds following in full cry. After skirting the shore of the loch, the fox ascended the eastern slope of Arthur's Seat, and ran to ground in a hole near the summit, which had not been previously known to any member of the hunt. It must have been an interesting sight to see the "field" toiling up the steep face of the hill.

The HEDGEHOG is found in considerable numbers in the district. This animal possesses a greater amount of shrewdness than most people give him credit for. It is not generally known that he climbs trees—at least, so far as we are aware, this has never yet been well authenticated. From observations made while keeping one in a walled garden, it has been discovered that hedgehogs undoubtedly climb trees; and from the circumstance of finding eggshells at the bottom, they evidently rob nests in bushes as well as on the ground. If one is confined in a garden where fruit-trees are against the wall, he is almost certain to effect his escape. We have known them to get out of one garden in this manner and find their way into another adjoining, where they were detained prisoners owing to there being no fruit-trees in it to facilitate their climbing. Hedgehogs are easily tamed, and make interesting pets, being exceedingly active in running about a house. When cold weather sets in they hide themselves, and hibernate, according to hereditary habit, in any secluded corner where they are not likely to be disturbed. We have known one thus lost in a garret for a couple of months; and it was only when the weather became mild that he was heard running about, and so discovered.

The MOLE is found here, as he is found generally throughout Scotland. With the exception of proving himself a troublesome neighbour to farmers, by throwing up earth and thereby destroying grass and grain crops, he is a most inoffensive creature. He is, moreover, not without some actual redeeming points, as nature has given him a commission to kill and keep down worms and beetles that might be otherwise prejudicial. He does not hibernate like the hedgehog, but his excursions are less frequent during winter. There are few if any animals more sensitive to vibration than the mole.

STOATS and WEASELS—the latter in considerable numbers—are still to be found in the district. In the spring and summer of 1888 we collected five hundred of these animals to transport to New Zealand, in order to form a natural check to the rabbits which are there increasing in inordinate numbers. While they were forwarded from all parts of Scotland, a few were taken from the environs of Craigmillar. Though, as indicated, stoats are rarer than weasels, still they are by no means extinct. Stoats are easily known from weasels by being larger, and from their black-tipped tails. In winter they change their coat from its normal brown colour to one of snowy whiteness, with the exception of the black tip on the tail. Weasels, on the other hand, never change their colour. Stoat skins form the valuable ermine fur of commerce, worn by royalty and the judges of our law-courts, and the animal is therefore also known as the ermine weasel. It is a notable fact, however, that stoats in this country have fur much inferior to those of Siberia or other northern regions, the fur of the British stoat having neither their thickness nor the same beautiful snowy whiteness. So recently as last year, when shooting in a field near Craigmillar, we noticed a stoat running in and out of an old stone wall, where he appeared to be amusing himself. To our surprise he was shortly thereafter seen about a hundred yards in advance, posting up the side of the wall with great speed. Knowing that the stoat had observed nothing to make him apprehensive of danger, we were curious to discover the motive by which he was impelled. Following in pursuit, it was interesting to observe that he occasionally raised his head in the air, as if attracted by the scent of prey. Having apparently measured his distance, he again pressed forward with increasing speed, as if forced on by some overpowering instinct. Although hitherto familiar with the movements of the stoat, we were not prepared for the alacrity with which he kept in advance. Latterly he seemed to become desperate with excitement, when a brood of partridges ran screaming from the side of the old stone fence right across the field. This movement on the part of the partridges appeared to surprise and disconcert the stoat, who halted as if in a difficulty as to his future action. Being by this time fairly within shot—as, in his anxiety to get among his prey, he was oblivious of our having been in pursuit—we fired, but immediately regretted doing so, as it would have been interesting to see how he would have met the unexpected contingency.

Squirrels are also to be found in the district, though, in the absence of pine woods, they are by no means plentiful.

Bats are numerous, but only three varieties—the common, the long-eared, and Daubenton's bat—are to be found in this locality. Some years ago, on looking into a hole in a very large ash-tree at The Inch, we discovered a cavity in the trunk of considerable size, the result of decay. A great number—if not hundreds, certainly many dozens—of bats, from a day old to adult size, were hanging by the hooked claws on their wings to the soft rotten wood which constituted the roof and sides of the cavity. Pocketing a few of the largest of them, we proceeded to hand them over to Mr Hope, naturalist, Edinburgh, but found, ere his premises were reached, that one of them had produced a family of five young. On the following day another one produced seven young. It was amusing to watch the little ones being suckled, and to mark the eagerness which they displayed in hanging

LONG-EARED AND DAUBENTON'S BATS.

on to the nipples of the breasts. They turned out to be Daubenton's bat, which had not been previously recorded in Mid-Lothian. Some of them may now be seen in the Edinburgh Museum of Science and Art.

Of Rodents there are the usual kinds, including hares, rabbits, voles, mice, shrews, &c. As a consequence of the extension of the town, the two first-mentioned are becoming scarce.

Hares.—Up till very recently Craigmillar was a favourite " meet " of the Mid-Lothian Harriers. From its elevated position, the top of the castle was a chosen resort of those interested in seeing the chase, and from it we once had an admirable opportunity of observing the marvellous instinct of the hare in doubling back on her track to throw the dogs off the scent. The chase had lasted some time when we descried the hare, a long distance in advance of the hounds, come into the field north of the castle. " Puss " galloped up the centre of the field, then suddenly stopped, sat up, and for a second listened with pricked ears to the distant " full cry " of the hounds. Instantly she wheeled round, and galloped back for a couple of hundred yards, exactly where she had come up; then, with a great bound to the side, she struck off at a right angle down wind, and speedily disappeared from view. Turning to observe the hounds and riders, we wondered if they would discover the manœuvre, or follow up to where the hare had doubled. We were not kept long in suspense, for, on the hounds getting through the hedge, they took up the double scent, giving tongue as if vying with each other which should be loudest. A number of ladies and gentlemen came galloping up, evidently enjoying the sport. In an instant the music of the hounds had ceased, horses were suddenly pulled up, and disorder and disappointment ensued. Must it be confessed that we ran down from the top of the castle and betrayed the secret of poor "Puss," which conscience whispered should have been kept sacred! Again the hounds were "full cry" on the trail, and we returned to the top of the castle to watch the remainder of the hunt. Several checks were made, and the hounds seemed baffled; but, unfortunately for the hare, some of the "field" or an onlooker would yell out a "tally-ho," and the chase continued. The instinct and cunning displayed by "Puss" were therefore of no avail; and struggling up the furrow of a ploughed field, the hounds "from scent to view" speedily terminated the chase.

Rats are exceptionally numerous in the environs of Craigmillar, and, from the revolution which has taken place in their haunts and habits by burrowing out in the fields, and the consequent loss to the farmer, they are now regarded as a modern plague. On the Craigmillar irrigation-farm, which lies between the castle and the city, rats are found in great numbers, living on the garbage which comes down the sewers, thus acting the part of the "scavengers of nature." The sewage is turned on to overflow a part of the meadow every day, three weeks being required to irrigate the entire area. With all their shrewdness and foresight, rats do not seem to anticipate the periodical inundation of the meadow, as they burrow, and sometimes breed, on the banks of the runnels. Last summer, while the sewage was being turned on from one part to another, we watched it first coming down the main carrier, then branching into, and commencing to trickle slowly down, the smaller ones. In the runnel near where we stood, a rat, discovering the water getting into her burrow, came out with something in her mouth, ran five or six yards, and then deposited her burden on a high part of the bank. She immediately returned to the burrow, and six times repeated the manœuvre. How many more times she intended returning must remain a mystery, as our two terriers, who regard the meadows as their "happy hunting-ground," and who had been rat-catching at some distance, came running up, as soon as they espied the rat. Her only refuge was in the burrow, but the ever-increasing volume of water caused her to bolt, when she was immediately seized and destroyed. It was then discovered that the rat had been engaged in carrying out her young, with the evident intention of conveying them to a place of safety,—a wonderful exhibition of the instinct and natural affection implanted within the breast of the much despised and persecuted rat.

The Vole.—Both the field vole and the water vole are to be found in the Craigmillar district, the latter frequenting the neighbouring brooks in large numbers.

The field vole is one of the most productive of this tribe of animals, and not unfrequently becomes a most destructive pest to the farmer. Unlike most animals of this species, they appear, strangely enough, to thrive

VOLES.

best in wet seasons, and on damp soil. About fifteen years ago the farmers in the pastoral districts of Selkirkshire had a visitation of this plague. Like the locusts of Egypt, whole mountain-sides and pastoral glens were literally covered with countless numbers of these creatures. So destructive were they to the vegetation, that the grass was completely eaten up and destroyed, and flocks of sheep had to be removed from certain districts because of the absence of food. In 1891 a similar visitation was experienced in Selkirkshire and adjacent counties, notably Dumfriesshire, Roxburghshire, and East Lothian. The extent to which this modern plague was experienced, because of their incalculable numbers and destructive habits, may be imagined on perusing the following well-authenticated testimony of shepherds and other reliable persons upon the spot. "The vermin have," says one informant, " multiplied greatly during the summer, and they now swarm in numbers which defy computation. To speak of them as in thousands, gives no idea of them." Another says: "It is impossible to speak too strongly about the plague, and unless one was to go over the ground, he could form no adequate conception of it." On certain farms which he specifies, this correspondent says, " they are simply legion." Another writes : "Nobody ever saw anything the least like it." It was remarked that the vermin did not live on the lea grasses, or dry hillsides; the grassy bogs and white bent were the places where they abounded most. Wherever the ground was what the shepherds speak of as "not bare," there they swarmed in greatest numbers. "They nibble and gnaw the long grass close to the ground, and the land is rendered altogether valueless for winter and spring feeding." Speaking of Eskdalemuir, another correspondent says: "The bog land on some of the farms is nearly ruined. Only a few sprat stalks stand here and there, but all the grass in the bottom, on which the sheep depend for winter food, is destroyed. Hundreds of acres of the best pasture land on many farms have thus for the present been totally destroyed, and whole hill-sides wear a blasted and desolate aspect, the ground being perfectly riddled by their holes and runs."

It is an interesting fact, but one which all well-informed naturalists will readily anticipate, that owls and kestrels increased greatly all over the infested region. One informant mentions that in his locality the latter "are as plentiful as crows, and in such an emergency all are gladly welcomed." To such an intolerable extent had this plague grown, that, among other expedients resorted to, cats were collected and let loose in large numbers, with the view of its abatement. In one district no fewer than upwards of fifty were turned adrift where there was shelter of whin and broom for them, but without any perceptible result.

The SHREW, the LESSER SHREW, the LONG-TAILED FIELD MOUSE, and the COMMON MOUSE, *Mus musculus*, are to be found in the Craigmillar district, as elsewhere.

REPTILES are represented in this locality by the blind-worm or slow-worm. In Leslie's 'Historie of Scotland,' the following passage occurs regarding the finding of two "scorpiouns" at Craigmillar Castle in the beginning of the sixteenth century. The historian says: "In the zaird of Craigmiller besyd Ed^r war fund tua scorpiouns, ane lyueng, the vther deid: quhilk scotismen held for sum foirtakneng nocht gude, feiret mony and ferliet, because in Brittannie was neuir a

Scorpioun seine afore."[1] This passage throws a lurid light on the credulity and superstition of the age—characteristics which, we fear, are not altogether extinct even in this more enlightened nineteenth century, now rounding to its close. In all probability the "scorpiouns" which caused such widespread terror at that time were harmless creatures—possibly the innocent blind-worm. Yet this incident seems to have been thought of sufficient importance to be noticed by another historian of that period in almost identical terms, namely, by Holinshed, in his well-known 'Chronicle.' This leads us to say that the blind-worm (*Anguis fragilis*) is found on the Braid Hills, as well as in many other parts of the country; and a specimen from the Braids was exhibited lately at a meeting of the Edinburgh Field Naturalists' Society. It is a perfectly harmless creature, its diet consisting of snails, worms, insects, &c., and it cannot even pierce the skin of a human being. From the fact of the muscles of its tail becoming stiffened to

---

[1] Leslie's 'Historie of Scotland' (Scottish Text Society ed.), Part III., p. 132.

such a degree, when the animal is alarmed, that the tail actually breaks off when seized by any one, it has received the specific name of *fragilis*.

LIZARDS.—While these creatures cannot be regarded as plentiful in this locality, they are by no means uncommon. We have frequently discovered them, on dissection of predatory birds, and notably magpies, doubled up in the gizzards.

Referring to the Amphibia, we may mention at the outset that the NEWT and FROG may both be included in the bill of fare of birds, wild ducks and herons especially. Frogs and newts are plentiful in the ponds on the Braid Hills, as well as at Dunsappie, Duddingston, &c. To our mind, there are few pets more interesting than newts. The male is easily known, at least in the breeding season, from the crest down the entire length of his back, as well as from his more brilliant colours. Transfer a worm into a glass globe beside a pair of newts, and as a rule each will seize an end and devour it till they come to close quarters, when a "tug of war" is almost certain to ensue. How they twist and wriggle round each other, both determined not to give way, till the difficulty is settled by the worm breaking asunder! If facilities are afforded them, newts will lay their eggs in captivity, which they do generally in April. The eggs do not adhere together, like the spawn of frogs, but each is deposited separately on a leaf and folded up by the mother. In due course the young newt issues from the egg, and, after passing through its various stages, reaches at length adult size. In keeping newts in confinement, care should be taken that an island formed by a stone or something similar be placed in the water, in order that they may have facilities afforded them for crawling to "land," which they readily take advantage of. The "island" must be in the centre, for if near the side they will speedily take their departure. Such was our experience when a dozen splendid specimens bade us good-bye in the summer of 1891. Awakened early by the screaming of a servant-maid, we hurried to the kitchen, thinking burglars had effected an entrance, and were not a little amused to discover that the alarm was caused by a couple of newts crawling about the kitchen-floor. So

A GROUP OF NEWTS.

terrified was the girl that, some hours after, her eye imperfectly caught sight of a clipping of black cloth in a corner, when she immediately screamed at the pitch of her voice and made for the door, declaring she would not stay in the house beside these "horrid brutes."

What has just been recommended regarding newts is equally applicable to frogs, namely, the rearing of them from the spawn until they reach some degree of maturity. No more interesting lesson in natural history could be found than in watching the various stages through which these animals pass—from the fish-like tadpole, with external gills, to the perfect lung-breathing animal. Of the longevity of frogs it is difficult to speak with any degree of certainty, it being always unsafe to rest any theory upon experiments which dissociate animals from their natural environment and place them under surveillance in captivity. A case is known of one living for eight years in confinement, when it came to an untimely end. In their native habitat frogs have many enemies, —foxes, otters, and snakes devouring them with great gusto; and, as already indicated, wild ducks and herons have a predilection for such dainties. Even when beyond the reach of these enemies, the life of a frog is a hazardous one, as fish, especially pike and trout, devour them greedily. We have seen a large *Salmo ferox* landed with a net in Loch Garry, in the stomach of which there were discovered five adult frogs. These big fish are most shy to tempt with a line; but taking the hint from the one just mentioned, we secured a frog, tied a double hook along his back by a thread round the armpits, and fixed it to eight or ten yards of line, on the end of which was a distended bladder. Putting out the frog in the centre of the loch, he was set off to "paddle his own canoe." The bladder drifted slowly before the wind, while we watched with interest for a considerable time, but saw nothing to indicate that the frog had been interfered with. Commencing to fish with the rod, we succeeded in securing some fine trout, but occasionally turned to watch the white bladder, now a long distance off, floating on the level surface of the lake. When quite a mile and a half distant, we discovered, on looking up, that the bladder had disappeared. Calling Angus the boatman's attention to the circumstance, we by-and-by saw it appear on the surface. Winding up the line, and seizing an oar each, we rowed rapidly down the lake. By the time the place was reached, the difficulty in dragging the bladder below the surface had so tired out the fish that it was a simple matter to cut the line from the bladder and secure it to the one on our rod. After rowing to the shore, a splendid specimen of the *Salmo ferox*, fourteen pounds in weight, was landed.

The COMMON TOAD is also found in the district. It is often kept by gardeners, being extremely useful in killing insects in greenhouses and garden frames. Like the frog, it passes the winter in a dormant state; and several cases are known of its living for a number of years. Pennant, in his 'British Zoology,' mentions a tame toad that lived for more than forty years, when it was killed by a raven. The stories current of toads living for centuries embedded in blocks of stone may safely be consigned to the region of myth.

The amount of ignorance which in this "enlightened age" prevails in many parts of the country regarding newts, frogs, and other amphibious animals, which are amongst the most innocent and inoffensive of God's creatures, is most remarkable. In rural districts it is quite common to find boys, and even grown-up people, destroying them wherever and whenever an opportunity presents itself, having been brought up in the belief that they are "poisonous." It might be well if School Boards would introduce small aquariums into our schools, in order that children could have opportunities afforded them of studying the life-history of such interesting creatures as the frog, the toad, and the newt.

A few words regarding the Fish to be found in the locality may fittingly close this chapter. Fish are naturally scarce in the environs of Craigmillar, in consequence of the absence of any appreciable extent of unpolluted water. Trout are found in the Braid Burn, and the brook south of the castle used to be the habitat of a considerable number; but the pollution from oil and shale works has practically destroyed them. Duddingston Loch contains pike, perch, and eels, but we have never known any of a large size. Nine pounds is the heaviest pike we have ever killed in it. Minnows and sticklebacks are found in the Braid Burn, and the latter are also present in the ponds on the Braid Hills. Sticklebacks make interesting pets, and we have had them in confinement for over four years at a time. They are very pugnacious, frequently attacking each other when first put together in the same vessel. They also make savage onsets upon any new comer to their private domain; and we have hit on the plan of separating the stranger from them, at first, by the introduction of a sheet of glass, until they become familiar with the presence of the intruder.

IV.

The Avifauna.

Having already given a description of the mammalian fauna, this work would be incomplete without a reference to the aquatic fowl and game birds of the district, and to those beautiful and inimitable songsters that enliven our woods and afford interest to our walks, shutting out solitude by the sweetness of their song. Notwithstanding its proximity to a large city, few districts have a richer variety of bird life than the environs of Craigmillar; and as a list of these birds may not be uninteresting, we here submit the following to our readers, commenting on each in turn.

The MALLARD DUCK is very plentiful. Being nocturnal in its habits, it is seldom seen in so thickly populated a district during the day, but at night large numbers frequent the brooks, the irrigated meadows, and Duddingston Loch. Notwithstanding their shyness, mallard soon become accustomed to any noise that does not threaten danger to them. We have frequently flushed them in the Braid burn at night close to a railway bridge where trains were thundering past every few minutes. Mallard are easily tamed when reared from the egg; and we have known them, when eight months old, walk fearlessly into a hen-house and drop their eggs.

The WIDGEON is a rare visitor to this district. Three years ago at Duddingston Loch we discovered a brace of widgeon feeding within shot of the shore, but at a place where there was little cover. The stalking of them was no easy matter. Anxious to acquire them for our collection, we wriggled like a serpent among the mud till within range, when we fired and brought them both down at a shot. The female was only winged, and, in spite of our best efforts to capture her, could not be secured, but the male was a splendid specimen.

The TEAL, though one of the commonest of ducks,

is by no means plentiful here. We have occasionally shot them in Duddingston Loch, in the Braid burn, and in Little France brook.

The LONG-TAILED DUCK rarely comes inland, but once we succeeded in shooting an immature female on Duddingston Loch.

LONG-TAILED DUCK.

The POCHARD is very common, and every year a good many are bagged at Duddingston Loch. This bird is supposed by some to be delicious—the flesh, it is asserted, resembling that of the celebrated "Canvas-back"; but, in our opinion, it is not to be compared to the mallard, teal, or widgeon.

The TUFTED DUCK is plentiful, and, except at breeding-time, a flock of them may be almost constantly seen on Duddingston Loch. An Edinburgh naturalist lately kept a pair of them as pets, which were very tame, and ate from his hand. They were hatched and reared by a small decoy duck. Tufted ducks occasionally breed in confinement.

GOLDEN-EYE DUCK are occasionally found, but not nearly in such numbers as they were some years ago. Old drakes are wide awake, and generally contrive to take care of themselves. Only once have we succeeded in securing one, though females and young birds are easily and frequently bagged.

The SCAUP DUCK is a common visitor in the spring months, large numbers frequenting Duddingston. They resemble the pochard, with this exception, that their heads and necks are black instead of brown.

The MOOR-HEN, or WATER-HEN as it is commonly called, is very numerous at the loch referred to. The same remark applies to the COOT. Both are extremely interesting birds.

The QUAIL, though no doubt rare, is occasionally found in the district. When partridge-shooting a few years ago in a turnip-field, the dog made a dead point, and a covey of seven quail rose on our approach.

The WATER-OUSEL is a most interesting bird, and is well known on all the streams in the neighbourhood. We are of opinion that it should be included in the singing class, as its low sweet note is frequently heard, even when the brooks are almost covered with ice.

The KINGFISHER, the most beautiful of all our British birds, is by no means uncommon near Craigmillar. They regularly frequent the Braid burn, and are strictly preserved by the proprietor. Last year we kept one in a cage, which was the most tame and interesting pet we ever had. It appeared to have no fear, and would sit on our

THE QUAIL.

finger in the presence of strangers with an air of the greatest unconcern. Nothing pleased us more than to see it fishing. Putting some live minnows or sticklebacks in a plate among water, it would dart down, quickly secure its prey, and before swallowing would kill it by beating it against the side of the plate, according to hereditary habit. Like most pets, this bird came to an untimely end.

THE PET KINGFISHER.

The CURLEW is seldom seen in the district, but while sitting on the wall of Craigmillar Castle some years ago, seven curlews flew over our head, when a gentleman fired and brought one down—an old cock, and a splendid specimen. Once or twice they have been seen on the irrigated meadows here.

The BARN OWL is frequently seen at Craigmillar.

Two years ago a farm-servant caught one sleeping in a field near the castle. Getting possession of it, we kept it in a kennel, where we made some experiments by shutting a live rat in beside it. It usually sat on a high shelf, and as the rat remained on the floor, the two did not interfere with each other. We were for a long time of the opinion that the owl never flew to the ground, but in this we had been mistaken, for shutting a badger in beside them, both rat and owl found their way into his capacious maw, much to our regret.

THE BARN OWL.

The TAWNY OWL is plentiful in the locality, and at certain seasons their eerie cries may be heard in all the woods surrounding Craigmillar. Though generally regarded as nocturnal in their habits, owls, when pressed by the cares of providing for a hungry brood, frequently commence to hunt for prey early in the afternoon. In the summer of 1891 we took three young tawny owls from the nest, and confined them in a box, with the view of discovering what kind of food the parent birds would bring to them. We found that young rabbits, mice, blackbirds, thrushes, chaffinches, yellowhammers, sparrows, and other small birds, were included in their bill of fare. It is dangerous for children to go near a nest containing young owls, numerous instances being recorded of the parent birds attacking and lacerating the body of the intruder. While out one evening in the gloaming with the object of shooting a few rats for some pet kestrels, we passed the box where the young owls were confined. After a few defiant threatenings from different trees, the male bird flew to attack us, making straight for the face. When within eight or ten feet, he seemed so resolute in his purpose that we threw the gun hurriedly upwards and backwards with the view of scaring or striking him, and protecting our face should he persist in his attack. Unfortunately, at that moment the female was approaching from behind, and as the gun was thrown quickly backwards, prior to bringing it down to strike the male, it met the female with such violence that it knocked her to the ground. She was only stunned, however, and quickly getting up, flew on to an adjoining tree. From the number of feathers on the ground and adhering to the muzzle of the gun, she must have been badly injured. For two days she was not once seen, but on the third day we were pleased to see her return to watch over her imprisoned progeny. The male bird did not actually touch our face, but being beaten off, he flew up into a tree overhead, and carefully scrutinised our proceedings.

The SHORT-EARED OWL, though rare, we have more than once flushed in turnip-fields when partridge-shooting. Though a few remain in this country the entire year, by far the greater number are migratory.

The LONG-EARED OWL, though the commonest of the species, is rare around Craigmillar. In the spring of 1891 we brought a young brood from Abington, in Lanarkshire, and after keeping them till fully matured, gave them their liberty.

The CARRION CROW, though no doubt rare, is found in the district. A pair make their nest every year in the policies of Prestonfield. The GREY CROW is seldom seen, but we have twice shot one in the Craigmillar woods. The ROOK, as in most parts of the country, is plentiful at Craigmillar. A number of rookeries exist within a mile of the castle. We have known a pair of rooks build their nest on a chimney of the Inch House.

JACKDAWS are numerous, as, with the exception of boys at nesting-time, few people care to molest them in this district. A number breed in the castle ruins. Though not often seen, albinos are yet occasionally met with. A naturalist of our acquaintance has a pair, the one pure white and the other buff-coloured, taken from the same nest last year.

The HERON is by no means rare, and may frequently be seen in the brooks south of the castle. At dusk it may also be observed winging its way towards

Duddingston to fish for perch, with which the loch abounds.

The Cuckoo visits Craigmillar, as it does most parts of Scotland, its arrival being welcomed as the harbinger of spring. In 1888 we were interested to observe that these birds were exceptionally numerous that season,

Cuckoo fed by a Wagtail.

as many as twenty being seen flying about at one time. Prompted by a desire to discover the cause of their increase, we shot one, and on dissection found the gizzard full of green caterpillars. As a large number of gooseberry bushes in an adjoining market-garden seemed blighted, we noticed on examining them that the leaves were being eaten by the grubs referred to. Watching with interest for eight or ten days, we observed the caterpillars gradually became scarcer, and the cuckoos shortly afterwards disappeared.

A friend, while botanising around Cobbinshaw Loch, discovered a young cuckoo, not quite fledged, in a wagtail's nest. Thinking to make a pet of it, he put it in his pocket with the intention of taking it home. Having some time to wait for a train, he turned up stones in search of insects, which he transferred into the gaping mouth of the cuckoo. It seemed insatiable, and before the arrival of the train he felt he had made a mistake in removing it from the nest, as to provide a sufficient number of insects to satisfy the bird seemed an impossibility. Anxious now to get rid of it, he, on reaching Edinburgh, handed it over to Mr Dewar, naturalist, St Patrick Square. That gentleman fed it exclusively with pease-brose, made with boiling water, and formed with the finger and thumb into oblong pellets, putting them into the bird's mouth when it gaped, which it did with great eagerness. After keeping it for a fortnight in this manner, an enthusiastic lady naturalist, the late

Mrs Hoyes of Skelmorlie, asked for the bird—a request which was readily acceded to. Putting the cuckoo into a large aviary, where, among many other birds, were American blue robins, she was surprised, when feeding it with meal-worms, and accidentally dropping one, to see a little blue robin pick it up, and at once pop it into the cuckoo's mouth. She subsequently observed that the same bird fed it regularly, and showed fight to any other bird that dared to come near it. Instances have occasionally been recorded of foster-mothers of cuckoos, in their wild state, starving themselves to death in their devotion to supply their gluttonous charge with food, when immediately a bird, sometimes of another species, would commence to provide for the young brood. These statements have naturally been accepted with reserve, but the case in point affords some corroboration of their accuracy. Mrs Hoyes wrote: "I don't know when I felt the loss of a pet more than I do the dear devoted blue nurse which we found dead this morning. I do most thoroughly believe that the poor wee bird starved itself to death in trying to keep the cuckoo satisfied with food. I have seen it pick up three mealworms at once when I threw in about a dozen, in the hope it might take one for itself; but no—every one he scrambled for went down the cuckoo's throat, never apparently swallowing one itself. Strange to say, one of the cardinals (Pope, South American) has taken charge of the cuckoo, and is feeding it well." Eventually it picked its food for itself, and up till the end of October seemed to thrive; but on the night of the 30th of that month several degrees of frost were encountered, and "the following morning," the lady wrote, "I saw at once he was doomed, but his end was so gentle that he really seemed to sleep away."

This incident affords another illustration of the futility of practising experiments where the natural instincts of the creatures involved and the law of adaptation are not fully considered. In few cases have we found experiments in natural history of the character here referred to succeed. So long as external circumstances constrain wild birds or animals to adapt themselves to their somewhat anomalous position, they will submit to it, but in the long-run nature generally asserts itself, and declines to be governed by artificial expedients.

MAGPIES are plentiful in the neighbourhood, and are most interesting though mischievous birds. They are very destructive to the eggs and young of game, as well as to birds of the singing class. They are long-lived, though reliable statistics of their longevity are difficult to acquire. A very amusing pet, locally known as the "Liberton Magpie," has been kept for a number of years now in semi-captivity, and as its history is interesting, a short account of this bird is here given.

In the spring of 1881 Mr Kerr, the postmaster at Liberton, found a young magpie which had dropped from a nest in the Kingston Grange wood, and was unable to fly. Taking it home, he attempted to feed it, but for two days it could not be induced to open its mouth. On the third day it was compelled by hunger to accept the proffered food, and after partaking of it, seemed at once to become reconciled to its new circumstances. In a short time it became very tame, and much attached to the postmaster's son. It followed him about wherever he went, and was his constant companion in the workshop. By-and-by "Jacky," as he is called, became very mischievous, and stole everything he was able to lift. All the small tools disappeared, but by watching his movements the hiding-place was found, and the stolen articles recovered. For some time the playing of marbles by boys on the road in the centre of the village had come to be a source of annoyance. "Jacky," however, soon put a stop to this. Quick as lightning he would dart down among the boys, pick up a marble, and fly off with it to his hiding-place. But the loss of their marbles was more

"JACKY," THE LIBERTON MAGPIE.

than the boys would stand, and "Jacky" was subjected to revengeful treatment; stones were thrown at him whenever an opportunity offered, with the result that he has had many narrow escapes, and one of his legs has been broken in two places. In spite of this, however, he has been the means of entirely putting a stop to boys playing marbles on the road. "Jacky" robs all the birds' nests in proximity to his premises, and is often besieged by blackbirds, thrushes, and other small birds, while he is amusing himself in tearing their nests to pieces or regaling himself on their eggs. Sometimes several of his own species appear within sight, when he instantly attacks them, and frequently returns ruffled both in feathers and temper. The only member of the feathered tribe with which "Jacky" seems to fraternise is a rook. For hours the two may be seen together sitting on the high trees that overhang the woodyard, or flying about, apparently without other aim than the enjoyment of each other's company. "Jacky's" mischievous tricks became so serious that he was at one time condemned to death. He had long been in the habit of flying at boys and grown-up people, but had never interfered with helpless children. One day, however, he flew at a child, and on the little fellow falling forward, he pecked the back of his head till the piteous screams brought the mother to the rescue. Such conduct could not be tolerated, and "Jacky," as already said, was condemned to suffer capital punishment. Hearing of the circumstance, we interceded on his behalf, with the result that his sentence was commuted to a couple of months' imprisonment in a cage. Whether his confinement had a beneficial effect, or whether, as he grows older, he is becoming endowed with more sense, we are unable to state, but he has now given up attacking children unless to defend himself when molested by them.

The GREAT SPOTTED WOODPECKER we have seen at Niddrie, in the policies of Duddingston, and at The Inch. At the latter place one remained for a long time in the summer of 1890. It is most interesting to watch the habits of this bird. After choosing a suitable cleft between two branches, it pecks a hole with its powerful beak, in which it tightly wedges fir cones, thus securing facilities for pulling them to pieces, one segment at a time, in order to get at the seed. An illustration of this came under our notice as we saw the bird feeding, and on climbing the tree the cone was found tightly wedged, while the fragments of others lay in profusion at the foot.

In 1890 a great spotted woodpecker for several weeks frequented the gardens in the village of Liberton, and eventually became entangled in a net for protecting strawberries from the depredations of blackbirds. Being secured by Mr Forbes of Craigievar, it was taken by that gentleman to Mr Dewar, naturalist, Edinburgh, with the view of having it stuffed. As it was still alive, Mr Dewar pled that the bird should be spared, a request which was readily granted. It was thereupon put into Mr Dewar's large aviary at the back of his premises in St Patrick Square, and was fed on American pea-nuts and insect food, which it seemed greatly to relish. Notwithstanding that it appeared to thrive, it did not become reconciled to being confined, and during the many months it was in the aviary it wrought almost incessantly to effect its escape. It made holes in the woodwork, and the harder the wood the better it seemed to like to peck at it. But for being closely watched, and the holes repaired, it doubtless would soon have made its exit. As far as its bill could reach in between the stones, it loosened the plaster from the wall, and, with the greatest amount of perseverance, pecked away at the iron bars incessantly. On the first Sunday of the bird's imprisonment a zealous policeman on the beat heard a noise in an ironmonger's shop adjoining Mr Dewar's premises.

THE GREAT SPOTTED WOODPECKER.

Listening at the keyhole, he concluded that burglars had effected an entrance, and were engaged in picking the lock of the safe. Raising the alarm, the premises were speedily surrounded by policemen, and a detective proceeded first to the proprietor's house and then to church, where Mr Dewar was, to bring him to the shop. On the door being opened no burglar was found, and it was ultimately discovered that the noise was caused by "ane o' Dewar's parrots," as some one dubbed the woodpecker, hammering away with his powerful bill against the bars of his prison. The destruction to the woodwork of the aviary became intolerable, and the bird was eventually confined in an iron cage. This mode of treatment, however, did not seem to agree with him, and he soon afterwards died, having been over twelve months in confinement.

The THRUSH, as might be expected, is very common around Craigmillar. The severe winter of 1880-81 almost annihilated them, and for several years afterwards they were exceedingly scarce. Now, however, they are again plentiful, and the ear is delighted by their soft and charming melody. The song of the thrush is among the first to be heard after the dull dark days of winter, and it is welcomed as one of the sweetest harbingers of spring.

The MISSEL-THRUSH, though not nearly so common as the preceding species, is nevertheless abundant. It is fond of fruit, and does no little mischief to strawberries in the Craigmillar market-gardens.

The FIELDFARE is generally regarded as the forerunner of hard weather, and is one of our most familiar winter visitors. Fieldfares are frequently seen in the district in large flocks.

The REDWING is also a winter visitor, and one which soon suffers from severe weather. During frost redwings flock in large numbers to the irrigated meadows, a part of which we always keep flooded in a storm, for the express purpose of feeding the birds which congregate there in thousands.

The BLACKBIRD is very common; and albinos and pied specimens are occasionally seen around Craigmillar.

A few WOODCOCK are shot here every season. We have never known them to nest in the environs of Craigmillar, though they do in many parts of England and Scotland.

SNIPE are plentiful, and at nights feed in large

numbers on the Craigmillar irrigation-farm. The shores of Duddingston Loch constitute perennial feeding-ground for these birds, and numbers are shot there every season.

The JACKSNIPE is only a winter visitor, arriving in September and taking its departure in April. A considerable number of them are annually shot about Duddingston Loch.

The LANDRAIL or CORN-CRAKE is common here. But for its discordant croaking note, few persons would ever be aware of its presence. While spending a holiday on the Island of Hitteren, in Norway, in the spring of 1889, we felt rather lonely in our walks in consequence of being unable to speak or understand the language. The crake of the landrail, however monotonous it may be considered, had a wondrous effect in cheering our spirits: we felt as if we had heard the voice of an old friend. After such a confession, it is rather hard to say that we have shot numbers of these birds in second-crop grass in September.

The WATER-RAIL is not nearly so common as

the landrail, but is frequently seen at Duddingston Loch.

The SPOTTED CRAKE is a rare visitor to this locality. In 1890 one was found on the road near Liberton, its death having evidently been caused by its flying against the telegraph wires.

The DABCHICK or LITTLE GREBE breeds every season at Duddingston Loch. For years we have tried to get a specimen of an adult male, but have not yet succeeded, though we have followed them for hours with a boat. So expert are they at diving, that before the boat could be got within shot of one, down he would go; and while rowing near the spot, and watching for his reappearance, he would be discovered far out of shot in the rear. A dabchick was found near The Inch recently, having also met its death by flying against the telegraph wires.

The GOATSUCKER or NIGHT-JAR, though unknown to many on account of its nocturnal habits, is found in this district. We have often seen one at dusk on a clothes-pole in the laundry green at The Inch.

The PEREGRINE FALCON we have twice seen at

Craigmillar. The BUZZARD we have only once observed, in the Hermitage wood. The OSPREY we noticed one Sunday evening in the spring of 1890 circling round Duddingston Loch, with the evident

THE GOATSUCKER OR NIGHT-JAR.

intention of alighting. Unfortunately a large number of people were about, and after flying round for five or six minutes, it winged its way towards the south-east.

The SPARROW-HAWK is frequently seen, and occasionally breeds about Craigmillar. It is more destructive to birds of the singing class and young game than any other of the hawk tribe. The number of bird remains found near sparrow-hawks' nests when they are rearing their young is almost incredible. In March 1887 a female sparrow-hawk dashed with great violence against the plate-glass window of Almora Villa, Liberton, then occupied by Mr Patrick Guthrie, and was picked up dead by that gentleman. It was not unnaturally assumed that the hawk had been in pursuit of its prey, though it was significant that there was no indication of any other bird having struck the window. Some days after, while Mr Guthrie was conversing with his gardener, he was startled by a sharp thud, as if something of a soft or flexible nature had been thrown against the window overhead. On looking up he was surprised to see a bird of considerable size falling to the ground. On picking it up he was interested to find that it was another sparrow-hawk, but on this occasion a male bird. Again it was conjectured that this hawk had met its untimely fate in pursuit of its prey. Our attention having been called to the fact, we felt convinced, after having carefully examined the place, that the hawks were not in pursuit of prey at all. This conclusion was confirmed by the circumstance that neither in this case, nor, as indicated, in that of the former, was there the slightest trace of any small bird having struck the window. How this strange incident is to be accounted for is a matter which will interest most naturalists. We naturally felt puzzled, but in looking straight towards the window from a distance, we discovered what to our mind was the true solution of the mystery. We observed that the trees in Mount Vernon wood were clearly and distinctly reflected in the plate-glass—so much so, that it appeared to those looking in to be like an avenue of trees, along which it is known hawks are often seen to skim. There can be no doubt that had the blinds of the window been down, no such remarkable incident would have occurred. This theory is corroborated by additional observations subsequently referred to.

The MERLIN we have frequently seen here, but have never known it to breed.

The KESTREL is by far the most common hawk we have in Scotland, and is often seen at Craigmillar. It is regarded as a friend by the agriculturist, as the number of mice it destroys is scarcely credible. At present we have three kestrels as pets, and unless compelled by hunger, they will not eat any birds. If a number of dead mice and sparrows are put down to them, the former are all devoured, and a day intervenes before they will touch the latter. On dissecting a kestrel, we discovered four mice and a number of beetles in its crop and gizzard. It is right to mention, however, that when they have to provide for their hungry nestlings, young grouse, partridges, pheasants, and other birds are frequently killed by them.

The LARK is plentiful in this district, though large numbers are captured annually by bird-catchers from Edinburgh. An amount of gross Sabbath desecration is continually perpetrated by bands of profligate "roughs" from the city thus plying their merciless work. During a recent winter, when the ground for weeks was covered with snow, most birds, but especially larks, were on the point of starvation, and were attracted in large numbers to any speck of black ground that was visible. The bird-catching fraternity, taking a mean advantage, cleared the snow off manure heaps, where they spread their nets and captured the birds wholesale, so that for several years thereafter the public ear in this district was rarely gratified by the unrivalled music of these aerial songsters. We have here a species of rascality which unfortunately neither farmers, the officers of the Society for the Prevention of Cruelty to Animals, nor the county police have power to interfere with. There is no law of trespass to protect the farmer, however much his crops may be trampled and destroyed, apart from the costly process of interdict; and bird-catching, as already indicated, does not come within the pale of the law. By the Wild Birds Protection Act, any one, however well intentioned, who takes a thrush or lark from its nest for a pet during the breeding season is liable to be punished; and yet in the winter months the despicable class referred to is allowed to capture our songsters wholesale without fear of legal consequences. That such a state of matters is allowed to exist is a blot on our legislature, and it is to be hoped that some humane member of Parliament may take the matter up, otherwise the extirpation of the lark, not to speak of other feathered favourites, may have at no distant date to be deplored.

Grouse we have shot on a stubble field at Craigmillar. It was, however, after a high gale from the south-west, when they had doubtless been blown from the Pentlands. Several gentlemen of our acquaintance have seen them on Arthur's Seat.

The Greylag Goose is common in Mid-Lothian, and they sometimes alight on the reservoir of the Liberton Water Company.

Golden Plover, after returning from their breeding haunts, frequent the fields around Craigmillar during the autumn and winter, feeding on the insect life found on grass fields, turnip fields, and ploughed land.

The Peewit or Lapwing is much more plentiful than the Golden Plover, and is to be seen here at all seasons, though large numbers migrate from the hills after having reared their young. This is one of the most harmless of our British birds. It is most interesting to watch them feeding, picking up worms and slugs off the ground. The bird is very common in all parts of the country, and, except for its eggs being gathered for the market, is rarely molested. It was otherwise a century ago, when country people expressed great dislike to it, and destroyed it wherever and whenever they had an opportunity. The reason alleged was that this bird, being by instinct led to flit about and scream near any one who obtruded on the solitude of its native wilds, helped to guide the king's troops in their pursuit of the Covenanters holding conventicles, by its being observed to hover over a particular spot. In the revised edition of the Bible, at Leviticus xi. 19, the "lapwing" has given place to the "hoopoe," the latter being now generally considered to be the correct rendering. It is somewhat gratifying to know that the lapwing need no longer be characterised as "unclean," though that stigma is now transferred to "the bird of beauty."

The BLACK-HEADED GULL is common here, as in all parts of the country. This bird is partly nocturnal in its habits, and we have frequently seen it flying about all night feeding on moths. Though adhering to the coast during winter, it retires inland to breed, generally on an island in some marshy lake. At Pallinsburn, near Coldstream, large numbers breed on the islands in the lake there, and form an attraction for naturalists from all parts of the country. Thanks to the proprietor, Mr Askew Robertson, they are preserved with scrupulous care.

The COMMON GULL is to be seen in large numbers following the plough at Craigmillar, eagerly snatching up worms and grubs as they are exposed to view.

The GREAT BLACK-BACKED GULL is also to be seen around Craigmillar. In summer this bird is most destructive to eggs and young game on hillsides which they frequent. During the lambing season they also do serious mischief. We are assured by shepherds that they attack and kill sickly lambs; and we have frequently seen them gorging themselves on the carcase of a dead sheep. It seems somewhat of an anomaly that this bird should have the benefit of the Sea Birds Protection Act.

With the HERRING GULL every one is familiar. It may not, however, be generally known that it is an enemy to the farmer: we have frequently seen it disgorge quantities of grain, along with large numbers of worms.

PHEASANTS are to be seen in the woods around Craigmillar. In the spring of 1892 a beautiful pheasant cock, in full flight, dashed against the drawing-room window of a gentleman's mansion near Craigmillar, and such was the force of the impact that, although the plate-glass of the window was a quarter of an inch thick, the bird penetrated it, and fell dead in the centre of the room. Five years previously, we are informed, another pheasant killed itself by dashing through the same window.

PARTRIDGES are also found in considerable numbers, as many as twenty brace having been killed in one day in the fields around the castle in recent years. It is a curious fact that this familiar bird gets completely bewildered if placed in other circumstances than those to which it is accustomed. During the severe storm of 1881 numbers flew into Edinburgh, no doubt in search of food and attracted by the black ground, when, on being chased by boys, they never attempted to use their wings, but fluttered helplessly about till they were captured.

WOOD-PIGEONS, though not in great numbers, are found in the environs of Craigmillar. A few pairs nest in the dense foliage of the lime-trees at The Inch, where they are allowed to harbour and breed without restraint. Their nests, however, are very frequently robbed by magpies. In one of these limes we have several times removed the eggs of the wood-pigeon, and deposited those of a tame one. Though the young birds were successfully reared, no sooner were they able to provide for themselves than they bade good-bye to the woods, and took up their abode in a dovecot close by.

The STARLING is numerous in the Craigmillar district, and may be seen feeding in large flocks in the irrigated meadows and grass fields. There are few birds more interesting than the starling, and it is equally at home in town or country. Though generally regarded as insectivorous, we have found their gizzard to contain both fruit and grain. Starlings may be seen feeding on the currant-bushes in the market-gardens around Craigmillar. They also seem to be passionately fond of "rowans," which they devour with great gusto. An animated discussion recently took place in one of our leading journals as to whether starlings were responsible for the partial disappearance of larks, by devouring their eggs. The arguments advanced in support of the contention that they were thus responsible appeared so convincing, that we resolved to try an experiment. In an old grass meadow numbers of broods of starlings fed daily, turning up the half dried cow-manure and devouring the insects exposed to view. With the aid of some boys, we collected several dozens of small birds' eggs of different kinds. Making a number of artificial nests among the grass where the cow-droppings appeared most plentiful, we deposited therein three, four, and in some cases five eggs, and from a distance watched the result. Mother starlings with their young broods came and stalked about with characteristic activity over the spots where the eggs were deposited, but in no case were these interfered with. While not regarding this as an infallible test, we consider it presumptive evidence that starlings are in no way responsible for the scarcity of the lark.

The SWIFT is plentiful at Craigmillar, and breeds in holes in the south front of the castle ruins. Most people wonder at the small hole they go in at, considering the size of the bird.

THE SWIFT.

The SWALLOW also frequents the district.

The SAND-MARTIN abounds, and bores in nearly every sandbank in the district, where it deposits its eggs. This must be a hardy bird, as sometimes severe weather is experienced after its arrival.

The HOUSE-MARTIN may be regarded as the greatest favourite among the tribe of swallows. Its arrival is, in general, welcomed, and protection accorded to it when nesting under the eaves. When, however, it insists on building its nest in the corner of a window, the swallow's notion of the fitness of things does not always commend itself to the cleanly housewife.

The GOLD CREST is much more common than is generally believed. This bird has been noticed in cold weather in some of the gardens at Newington.

The COLE TIT, though common in all parts of the country, is not seen in great numbers around Craigmillar, being partial to fir plantations.

The BLUE TIT is very common. The female is most ferocious in her attacks upon any intruder approaching her nest.

The GREAT TIT is plentiful in this district, as in most parts of the country.

The LONG-TAILED TIT, though not in great numbers, is seen around Craigmillar, and sometimes in gardens in Edinburgh. The nest of this bird is well known to the juvenile egg-collector.

The TREE-CREEPER is often seen running up and round the trunks of the old elm and ash trees in the policies at The Inch.

JENNY WREN and COCK ROBIN are known everywhere, Craigmillar being no exception.

The SEDGE-WARBLER frequents, and occasionally breeds among, the reeds at Duddingston Loch. The nest is generally near the water, among the roots of the sedges, or against stumps of old trees beside the reeds. It is, however, almost impossible for this or any other bird, including the swans, to hatch their eggs or rear their young at Duddingston, so closely and carefully are their nests daily sought for by juveniles, as well as by "roughs" from the city. In point of fact, the provisions of the Wild Birds' Protection Act, so far as the neighbourhood of Edinburgh is concerned, may be regarded as a dead letter. Though not remarkably melodious, the sedge-warbler sings vigorously, commencing when the sun gets low, and, when the days are at their longest, sometimes continuing the entire night. As a consequence, paragraphs appear from time to time in the newspapers announcing that the nightingale has been heard in Scotland,—a statement which has always been found to be imaginary when the place was visited by any practical ornithologist.

The BLACKCAP is a summer migrant arriving in the spring, and leaves as soon as its young are sufficiently strong to provide for themselves. Though we have never seen it in close proximity to Craigmillar, it is frequently observed within a few miles' distance. The same remarks apply to the GARDEN-WARBLER.

The CHIFFCHAFF, though rare, we have seen in the district. It is usually the first of the warblers to visit us in the spring.

The WHITETHROAT is often seen on Arthur's Seat and on the hedges all round. This little migrant soon makes its arrival known by singing on the top of the first hedge it alights upon after reaching our shores. It is in beautiful plumage when it arrives, but soon assumes a very shabby appearance.

The WOOD-WARBLER is fairly plentiful, and generally found in tall woods. Numbers frequent the high beeches in Kingston Grange park.

The WILLOW-WARBLER is common in this locality.

The PIED WAGTAIL is plentiful around Craigmillar. Though a few of these birds remain with us over the winter, by far the greater number only visit us in summer. Like swallows, they congregate in particular places prior to their departure. Under the eaves of the General Post-Office in Edinburgh appears to be a favourite roosting-place after they assemble in flocks.

The WHITE WAGTAIL, though not common, is occasionally seen in the locality. It is not easily distinguished from the pied species, and considerable doubts exist among naturalists as to whether it is a true species or only a Continental form of the Pied Wagtail.

The GREY WAGTAIL is common. A pair nested recently in a hole in the wall of the old mill at Nether Liberton, behind the water-wheel. How they got out and in, when the wheel was in motion, is a mystery, as no one was ever able to see them make the attempt.

The TREE-PIPIT is only a summer visitor. It is fairly numerous in the woods around Craigmillar.

The MEADOW-PIPIT is one of the commonest of our birds. Though a few remain with us over winter, large numbers arrive from other countries in the spring.

The ROCK-PIPIT is also common near the coast, but has, as its name implies, a predilection for rocks on the sea-shore.

The SNOW-BUNTING is a winter migrant, and in severe winters is observed on Arthur's Seat.

The REED-BUNTING is not numerous, but occasional specimens are seen on marshy spots in this locality.

The CORN-BUNTING frequents the fields in the environs of Craigmillar.

The YELLOWHAMMER is found here at all seasons.

The HOUSE- and HEDGE-SPARROW are both very common.

The GREENFINCH is very plentiful. In September flocks of several thousands may be seen feeding on the oat stubbles around Craigmillar.

The SISKIN is a winter visitor, and large flocks are occasionally to be seen in the district.

The REDPOLE is by no means uncommon in this

locality, and is not unfrequently met with on the Braid Hills.

The LINNET does not appear to be so plentiful as it was in our bird-nesting days. Some are, however, still to be seen on Arthur's Seat and the Braid Hills.

The CHAFFINCH, though partially migratory, as is evidenced by numbers of them being killed by flying against the lighthouse lamps both in spring and autumn, is plentiful at all seasons around Craigmillar.

CHAFFINCH, BULLFINCH, AND CROSSBILL.

The BULLFINCH used to be plentiful in the locality. Thanks, however, to the bird-catching fraternity, they are now seldom seen.

The CROSSBILL may be considered a very rare bird. though a specimen turns up now and then. One was recently killed on Corstorphine Hill.

The GOLDFINCH we have seen occasionally about Craigmillar. A pair frequented the avenue at The Inch for some time a few years ago.

The COMMON SANDPIPER visits us in summer, frequenting the Braid burn and other brooks.

The SPOTTED FLYCATCHER is by no means plentiful, but specimens are to be observed. They seldom arrive till the middle of May, and leave early in autumn.

The RING-OUSEL is a summer migrant. We have often seen it on the Pentlands.

The REDSTART is a handsome little bird, and up till very recently bred on Blackford Hill. Now, however, that the hill has become the property of the citizens of Edinburgh, a bird's nest is as difficult to find there as the proverbial "needle in a haystack."

The Whinchat is found widely distributed over the country during the summer months, an occasional specimen being seen in this locality.

The Stonechat, though partially migratory, is found in Scotland during the entire year. A few are seen occasionally on Arthur's Seat.

The Wheatear, also a summer migrant, breeds on Arthur's Seat and the Braid Hills.

Most of our readers who have examined the foregoing list will now admit that we have made good the statement at the beginning of this chapter, that the Craigmillar district is peculiarly rich in bird-life. To city dwellers especially, it is very pleasant and refreshing to escape for a brief season into the country, and to have the wearied mind soothed by the varied music of our feathered songsters. The citizens of Edinburgh may be said to possess exceptional advantages in this respect; and not the least charming of their rural walks may be found in the environs of Craigmillar, where such "concert of sweet sounds" can be so fully enjoyed.

V.

Botany of the Craigmillar District.

Owing to the natural diversities of the landscape in the surroundings of Craigmillar, the flora of the district is at once rich and varied. Here are found height and valley, wood and meadow, marsh and lake, each with its characteristic vegetation. The peaks and precipices of Arthur's Seat and Salisbury Crags, the waters of Duddingston Loch and its fenny margin, the cultivated fields and plantations around Craigmillar, and the ruins of the ancient pile itself,—all these combine to furnish, in a comparatively small extent of surface, a remarkable number of our native plants. Many of these are, of course, the familiar friends that greet the lover of our British wild-flowers in many parts of the country; yet several of them are rare enough to make us hope they may long continue to thrive in the places where they have for so long found a congenial home.

The flora of Arthur's Seat and the country immediately surrounding has long engaged the attention of local botanists. The first list of plants found in these localities was drawn up by Sir Robert Sibbald, one of the founders of the Edinburgh Royal Botanic Garden, so early as 1684, and contained 881 species and varieties of flowering-plants; while about a century later Mr Yalden, assisted by a few other enthusiastic field-botanists, compiled a list of 313 species of plants, mostly growing on Arthur's Seat or Salisbury Crags, for Dr Lightfoot, who was then amassing material for his 'Flora Scotica,' the first edition of which appeared in 1777. With the exception of an additional list of Edinburgh plants, which was drawn up by a well-known authority, Mr R. Maughan, and published in the first volume of the Wernerian Society's Transactions for 1808-10,[1] no other catalogue of local plants

[1] The title of this interesting paper is, "A List of the Rarer Plants observed in the Neighbourhood of Edinburgh." By Robert Maughan, Esq., F.L.S. (Read 9th Dec. 1809.)

appeared till 1824, when Dr Greville produced his
'Flora Edinensis.' This now classic work is a bulky
volume of nearly 500 pages, and embraces both
flowering and flowerless plants, arranged under 1794
species. The need of a smaller and more portable
book called forth, a few months after the appearance of Dr Greville's work, a pocket volume entitled
'A Catalogue of the Indigenous Phenogamic Plants
growing in the Neighbourhood of Edinburgh, and
of certain Species of the Class Cryptogamia, with
Reference to their Localities,' by James Woodforde,
a prizeman at that date in the botanical class of
Professor Graham. This concise list of 806 species,
arranged according to the Linnæan system, as was
the fashion of the time, is still valuable, furnishing
a very interesting record of the plants then growing on
Arthur's Seat and within the precincts of the Park,
although the author goes occasionally much farther
afield. As a pocket companion for the field-botanist
in this district, it had no rival, for nearly forty
years, until, in 1863, it was superseded by the
'Flora of Edinburgh,' compiled by Professor J. H.

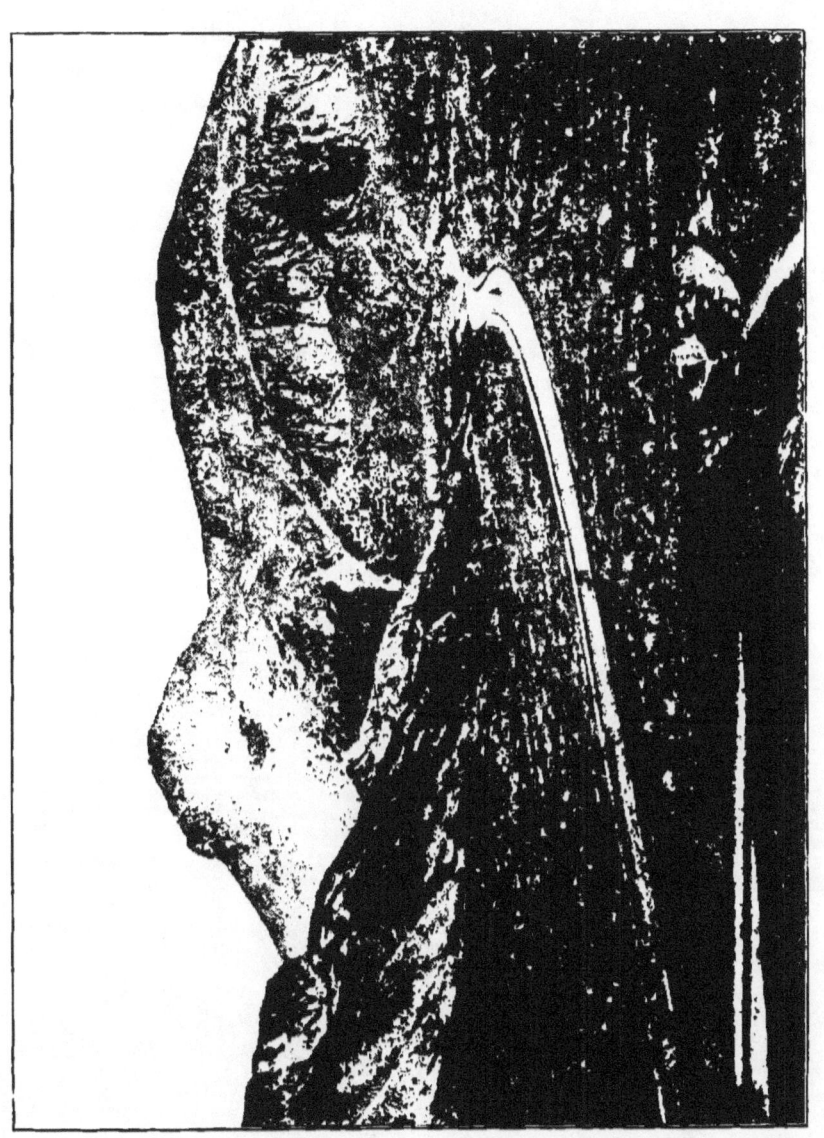

Arthur's Seat and Queen's Park.

Balfour and Mr John Sadler. Since the publication of this work, now more than a quarter of a century ago, no other book of the kind, dealing with our local plants, has appeared, though, from the extension of the city, and various other causes, numerous changes in the localities of plants have occurred during the interval. Many wild-flowers, also, which at a comparatively recent period were abundant within the precincts of the Park or in the surrounding district are now either almost eradicated or have entirely disappeared. As examples, the following amongst others are noted in Woodforde's Catalogue as growing at that time in the Hunter's Bog — viz., the Grass of Parnassus (*Parnassia palustris*), the nearest station for which is now the Pentlands; the lovely little Bog Pimpernel (*Anagallis tenella*), mentioned under the same locality in Professor Balfour's 'Flora,' but which is not now found nearer than Gullane and a few other distant stations; the Butterwort (*Pinguicula vulgaris*), which must also be now sought for on the Pentlands; and the Buckbean and Ragged Robin or Cuckoo-flower, which are both, happily, still growing near Duddingston Loch, but have long since vanished from the Hunter's Bog. Many other fine plants have left their old homes, such as the Wood Hyacinth and the Maiden Pink, and we can only heave a sigh over their loss. It is related of at least one enthusiastic botanist, who lamented this sad state of matters, that he was in the habit of filling his pockets with seeds of his vanished favourites, and sallying forth to the Park to scatter them broadcast over the heights and valleys. Numbers of our commoner native plants, however, are yet growing here; and the diligent searcher among the nooks and crannies may be rewarded by finding even some of what must now be termed the rarer kinds.

In attempting to enumerate the plants of the Craigmillar district, it will not only be necessary to circumscribe somewhat the area, but those plants also more commonly met with must, in a work of this kind, be almost entirely left out of account. Appended to this chapter will be found a list of plants which have been selected as less or more characteristic of the varied natural features of the district. As in many other "select lists" which have been drawn up, some may be surprised at finding certain names included, and others—it may be their own special favourites—left out. In all such cases one can only crave indulgence, and plead in extenuation the difficulty of the task. A general idea may now be given of the floral wealth of the included area, by special reference to some of what may be termed the outstanding plants.

Beginning with Craigmillar Castle, one or two plants which have possibly been connected with its occupation by Queen Mary, or by others at a somewhat later date, may be noted. Thus on the walls of the old building there is still found a pot-herb known as "French Sorrel" (*Rumex scutatus*), which may have been used by the cooks of the royal household, and thus got a footing here. This plant, however, though now found in several parts of Scotland and the North of England, and often connected with monkish culture, is not native. Another plant formerly used for culinary purposes is growing near the walls of the castle, namely, the Sweet Cicely (*Myrrhis odorata*). Both the popular and the scientific names of this "herb" have a certain poetic ring about them; and the whole plant is remarkable for its aromatic flavour. Though the Sweet Cicely is found in a few other localities in the neighbourhood of the city, generally near old dwellings or ruinous places, another Craigmillar plant is somewhat rare in our native flora, and is found nowhere else in the Edinburgh district. This is the plant known, curiously enough, as Alexanders (*Smyrnium olusatrum*), the young shoots of which were at one time, and perhaps are still in some places, used for the table. Though found here so far inland, this plant usually frequents waste ground near the seacoast. Of these three Craigmillar plants, only one— the Sweet Cicely—is noted by Dr Greville as growing in this locality in his time, though Woodforde gives Craigmillar Castle as a station for Alexanders. One is almost forced to believe that these authorities left the French sorrel out of their lists intentionally, from the fact of its being a straggler from cultivation, as common tradition now connects it with the name of Queen Mary. To this list of "pot-herbs" perhaps another should be added, namely, the plant known popularly as Good King Henry (*Chenopodium Bonus-Henricus*), also found at Craigmillar. The large succulent leaves of this plant are used in the same way as the common or garden spinach, belonging to the family of the Chenopodiaceæ, or Goosefoots, as does also Good King Henry, Orach, Beet, &c. All these plants are usually found naturalised near places that have at one time been used for human habitations.

A plant not very widely distributed in the Edinburgh district, though common in other places, is growing abundantly in the joints of the old masonry at the castle, namely, the Common Wall Pellitory (*Parietaria officinalis*). The Creeping Cinquefoil (*Potentilla reptans*), somewhat local in its character, is also still found here, but more sparingly than it once was. That lovely member of the Borage family, the Evergreen Alkanet (*Anchusa sempervirens*), is noted by Mr Neill as growing at Craigmillar Castle in 1799, and this is just the place where one would expect to find it. Though it has now become rather rare, and in some seasons scarcely a single plant of it can be found, yet it still maintains its ground to the south of the castle. Many of our common wildlings have, however, long since established themselves on the walls and amongst the ruins, and may always be found at their proper periods, as the Thyme-leaved Sandwort, the Vernal Whitlow Grass, the Dove's-foot Crane's-bill, the Wall Speedwell, the Black Knapweed, the Wall Hawkweed, &c. The pretty Mountain Crane's-bill (*Geranium pyrenaicum*), not very often met with, is still growing near the castle. So also is the Common Mallow, with its bright purple flowers, and the common Comfrey, a handsome plant, from two to three feet high, with clusters of drooping flowers.

In the Queen's Park, on Arthur's Seat, and on Salisbury Crags are yet growing a few plants which are well worth a passing notice. One beautiful wildflower, which, fortunately, from its position on the cliffs, it will be difficult to root out, is the German Catchfly (*Lychnis Viscaria*). A writer in the 'Scotsman,' over the signature of " Botanist," drew attention a short time ago to this plant, and to other floral features of the district, in the following terms: " One of the most charming sights in the vicinity of Edinburgh, in the way of a natural rock-garden on a large scale, is to be seen at present [in the month of June] in the Queen's Park, at Samson's Ribs. The basaltic rock itself—a geological phenomenon of great interest—is always an impressive object, but as one passes along, the eye is arrested by masses of the beautiful German Catchfly (*Lychnis Viscaria*) growing in luxuriance on the face of the rock, and lighting it up with its pink flowers. In contrast with it there is also the bright yellow Bird's-foot Trefoil (*Lotus corniculatus*), which tends to heighten the effect. . . . On the road farther east, towards the Windy Goul, overlooking Duddingston Loch, the green turf is jewelled with the handsome yellow petals of the Rock-rose (*Helianthemum vulgare*), a most attractive plant; while on the upper road—the Queen's Drive—the rocks during summer are always gay with the most beautiful of our wild plants, including Foxgloves, wild Geraniums, Spiræa, Teucrium, Milk-vetch (*Astragalus*), and others, reminding one of a good district in the Highlands." It is not only on a midsummer's day, however, that Flora's treasures are thus spread out here to view, for each season reveals its own special beauties—whether it be the budding time of the year,—

> " When Daisies pied and Violets blue,
> And Lady-smocks all silver-white,
> And Cuckoo-buds of yellow hue
> Do paint the meadows with delight;"—

or more sober autumn, with its knapweeds and thistles and wild grasses. One little gem of spring, said to be only found in a few places in Scotland and at the Lizard Point in Cornwall, is here so abundant as to merit particular notice. This is the Vernal Sandwort (the *Arenaria verna* of Linnæus)—a tiny plant, seldom more than three or four inches high, with comparatively large, white, star-shaped flowers, which bespangle the turf in spring-time and early summer. It is mentioned by Lightfoot as growing abundantly on Arthur's Seat in his time, and no doubt flourished in the same locality long before that period.

Any general notice such as this of the flora of Arthur's Seat and Salisbury Crags would be incomplete without reference to what is now widely known in botanical circles as "the Arthur's Seat fern." This fern, the Forked Spleenwort (*Asplenium septentrionale*), is thus noticed by Woodforde in 1824: "Basaltic columns in the King's Park, and frequent in many other places in the King's Park; rocks on the south side of Blackford Hill, abundant." It goes without saying that this delightful state of matters no longer subsists. In these days of fern mania it is only in a few inaccessible places on Samson's Ribs that the Forked Spleenwort continues to live; and though still found on the Braids, it is destined, no doubt, soon to share the same fate there.

Mention may now be made of some of the more noteworthy plants growing at or near Duddingston Loch. The first to claim attention is the Buckbean or Bogbean (*Menyanthes trifoliata*), already mentioned as found in this locality. This is undoubtedly one of the handsomest of our native plants, with its buds of a deep rose hue, and its corolla, when expanded, thickly fimbriated or fringed on the inner surface. It is to be devoutly hoped that it may long continue to thrive here, and not be trampled out of existence by cattle, as it now bids fair to be in the near future. Another somewhat rare plant, which may also suffer from the same cause, is the Glaucous Stitchwort (*Stellaria glauca*), which affects marshy ground, and has long found a home in this locality. It is mentioned by Mr Maughan, in his list of rare plants in the neighbourhood of Edinburgh already referred to, as growing here and at Lochend in the beginning of the century. The visitor to Duddingston Loch in the month of July, or thereabouts, might pass by this humble Stitchwort unnoticed, but could hardly fail to observe the handsome, tall, sword-shaped leaves and bright yellow flowers of the Water Iris (*Iris Pseud-acorus*), which forms quite a feature in the landscape at that time of the year. Another elegant plant, which at one time was conspicuous about the same season, but is now becoming very scarce here, is the so-called Flowering Rush (*Butomus umbellatus*), a rather rare plant, with its umbels of large rose-coloured flowers, introduced at some former period, though noted in this locality by Dr Greville and other early botanists. The Common Reed (the *Arundo Phragmites* of Linnæus), which adorns the sides of the loch with its tall stems and beautiful inflorescence, is also well worth notice. With the exception, perhaps, of Lochend, the Common Mare's-tail (*Hippuris vulgaris*) is found nowhere else in the Edinburgh flora except in Duddingston Loch, where it is abundant. Some good plants have disappeared from the loch through the cleaning out of the too luxuriant vegetation, or other causes. Thus the Water-Soldier (*Stratiotes aloides*), noted both by Mr Maughan and the late Professor Balfour as growing here, has now been lost.[1] Several species of Water-Crowfoot are, however, still present; and the Marsh Marigold, belonging to the same family as the Crowfoots, is very conspicuous in the early summer months, with its dark-green leaves and golden-yellow flowers. Last —and least—the ubiquitous tiny Duckweed, or Water

[1] It may be mentioned that this introduced plant has thoroughly established itself in an old marl-pit near Davidson's Mains, now filled with water, where it promises soon to choke out all other vegetation.

Ivy (*Lemna*), is at some seasons very plentiful, forming almost a green scum on the surface of the water. There are said to be no fewer than four different species of this diminutive plant found here, but only experts can determine them.

As somewhat connected with the botany of Craigmillar, a short notice of what is known as the "Craigmillar Sycamore" may not inappropriately close this chapter. This venerable Sycamore (*Acer pseudo-platanus*) stands at the foot of the hill near the castle, beside the hamlet of Little France. It is often called "Queen Mary's Tree," from the belief that it was planted by the queen during her residence at Craigmillar. There is no record, indeed, of her having done so, but the statement has been handed down by oral tradition, and as such the tree has been visited for generations by tourists from all parts of the world. A lady long resident in the district informs us that, when a girl, she frequently visited the tree under the care of a grand-aunt, who, if she were still alive, would now be about a hundred and fifty years of age. The belief at that time was, that Queen Mary planted the tree in the presence of Rizzio.

Some one, still inclined to be sceptical on the subject,

QUEEN MARY'S TREE.

might fairly reply to this, in the words of Sir Walter

Scott's "Antiquary," that "it may be only a lie with a circumstance." Still, assuming that the old lady referred to had the tradition, in all likelihood, handed down to her, the fact is at least established that Queen Mary's reputed connection with the tree is by no means a modern invention.

About a dozen years ago this Sycamore tree showed certain indications of decay, and fears were entertained that it might succumb to a high westerly gale. After consulting the best authorities, the late Mr Little Gilmour, with great reluctance, in September 1881 had the upper branches sawn off, in order that the tree might thus offer less resistance to the wind, and so ensure a likelihood of preserving it. As the branches fell to the ground, a large crop of seed was shaken off, which was carefully gathered, and sown in a neighbouring nursery. The tree received a great addition to its popular fame in 1886, when her Majesty, driving past it on her way to Dalkeith Palace, expressed a wish that it should be protected with an unscalable iron fence, which desire was readily acceded to by the proprietor.

This little incident finding its way at the time into the newspapers, requests came from all parts of the world for seedlings from "Queen Mary's tree." It was gratifying to all concerned that every application could be granted, as an abundant supply of young plants had grown from the seeds referred to above. At the request of her Majesty, a number of seedlings were also forwarded to Windsor and Balmoral, and not a few have since been planted to adorn portions of the Craigmillar estate. Among places of interest to which specimens were sent may be mentioned one which was planted beside the historic church of Ladykirk by the late Lady Marjoribanks; and another was placed within the shadow of the ruined walls of Linlithgow Palace, the birthplace of the unfortunate queen herself. On the occasion of the freedom of the burgh of Linlithgow being conferred upon the Right Hon. the Earl of Rosebery, that distinguished nobleman, in planting the seedling, spoke thus to a large assemblage: "We do not plant this tree in anything but a kindly spirit to that queen. If she was greatly sinning, she was yet, I think, more greatly sinned against; and her memory will always be interesting to the whole of humanity, and always an affectionate one to the people of this ancient burgh." A metal tablet fixed in the ground at the foot of the tree bears the following inscription: "This seedling from Queen Mary's Tree, growing at Little France, Craigmillar, was presented to the burgh of Linlithgow by Walter James Little Gilmour of Craigmillar, and, by permission of H.M. Board of Works, was planted by the Right Hon. the Earl of Rosebery, on 24th Sept. 1886, near the place in which Queen Mary, who planted the parent tree, was born." Perhaps this seedling, standing in this historic spot amid associations so intimately connected with the history of the Stuart race, when grown to stately proportions may prove an interesting memento to future generations of Scotland's beautiful but unfortunate queen, with her "Iliad of woes," when the parent tree from which it sprang has, by time or fate, been levelled with the ground.

LIST OF A FEW OF THE NATIVE PLANTS

FOUND IN THE CRAIGMILLAR DISTRICT—

Including Craigmillar, Duddingston, Arthur's Seat, Salisbury Crags, and Queen's Park.

Natural Order **Ranunculaceæ**—Buttercup Family.

1. *Ranunculus aquatilis* L., Common Water Crowfoot. Duddingston Loch; also several varieties of this plant.
2. *Ranunculus hederaceus* L., Ivy-leaved Crowfoot. On margin of loch; very dwarf.
3. *Ranunculus sceleratus* L., Celery-leaved Crowfoot. On margin of loch, abundant.
4. *Ranunculus Flammula* L., Lesser Spearwort. Common all round the loch.
5. *Ranunculus Lingua* L., Great Spearwort. Mostly on south side of loch, not very abundant.
6. *Caltha palustris* L., Common Marsh Marigold. Abundant on south side of loch.

Natural Order **Papaveraceæ**—Poppy Family.

7. *Papaver Rhœas* L., Common Red Poppy. Abundant in cornfields and waste places in the district.

NATURAL ORDER **Fumariaceæ**—Fumitory Family.

8. *Fumaria officinalis* L., Common Fumitory. Common all round the Park.
9. *Fumaria capreolata* L., Rampant Fumitory. Common in fields and waste places in the district.

NATURAL ORDER **Cruciferæ**—Cresswort Family.

10. *Cardamine pratensis* L., Meadow Bitter-Cress or Lady's Smock. Plentiful round margin of loch in spring.
11. *Sisymbrium Alliaria* Scop., Jack-by-the-Hedge. Dry places in the Park in spring.
12. *Sisymbrium officinale* Scop., Common Hedge-Mustard. In Park, abundant.
13. *Sisymbrium thalianum* Gaud., Common Thale-Cress. In Park, abundant.
14. *Cheiranthus Cheiri* L., Common Wallflower. Craigmillar Castle.
15. *Sinapis arvensis* L., Charlock or Wild Mustard. Unhappily only too common in corn-fields in the district.
16. *Barbaræa vulgaris* R. Br., Yellow Rocket. Abundant in the district.
17. *Draba verna* L., Common Whitlow-grass. Craigmillar Castle.

NATURAL ORDER **Cistineæ**—Rock-rose Family.

18. *Helianthemum vulgare* Gaert., Common Rock-rose. Generally distributed in dry rocky places on Arthur's Seat and Salisbury Crags.

NATURAL ORDER **Caryophylleæ**—Chickweed Family.

19. *Silene inflata* Sm., Bladder Campion. In the Park, not common.
20. *Lychnis Viscaria* L., German Catchfly. Samson's Ribs.
21. *Lychnis Flos-cuculi* L., Ragged Robin. Margin of loch, common.
22. *Sagina procumbens* L., Procumbent Pearlwort. In the Park, common.
23. *Arenaria verna* L., Vernal Sandwort. In perfection on southern slopes of Arthur's Seat; rare and local.
24. *Arenaria serpyllifolia* L., Thyme-leaved Sandwort. Craigmillar Castle and Park.
25. *Stellaria glauca* With., Marsh Stitchwort. East side of loch.
26. *Stellaria uliginosa* Murr., Bog Stitchwort. Margin of loch in some places.
27. *Cerastium arvense* L., Field Chickweed. Arthur's Seat, very sparingly.

NATURAL ORDER **Malvaceæ**—Mallow Family.

28. *Malva sylvestris* L., Common Mallow. Craigmillar.

NATURAL ORDER **Hypericineæ**—St John's Wort Family.

29. *Hypericum quadrangulum* L., Square-stalked St John's Wort. West side of loch, on wet ground.
30. *Hypericum pulchrum* L., Small upright St John's Wort. Arthur's Seat.

NATURAL ORDER **Geraniaceæ**—Crane's-bill Family.

31. *Geranium pratense* L., Blue Meadow Crane's-bill. Queen's Park.
32. *Geranium sanguineum* L., Bloody Crane's-bill. South side of Park; one of the prettiest of our native geraniums.

33. *Geranium molle* L., Dove's-foot Crane's-bill. Common at Duddingston.
34. *Geranium pyrenaicum* L., Mountain Crane's-bill. Craigmillar and Salisbury Crags. Not plentiful.
35. *Geranium Robertianum* L., Herb Robert. Near old walls and stony places, very common in district.
36. *Erodium cicutarium* Sm., Hemlock-leaved Stork's-bill. South side of Park.

NATURAL ORDER **Leguminosæ**—Pea and Bean Family.

37. *Ulex europæus* L., Common Furze or Whin. East side of Park.
38. *Ononis arvensis* L., Rest-Harrow. Duddingston and Queen's Park, in dry places.
39. *Trifolium arvense* L., Hare's-foot Trefoil. South side of Park.
40. *Trifolium procumbens* L., Hop Trefoil. Duddingston, in dry places.
41. *Lotus corniculatus* L., Bird's-foot Trefoil. Arthur's Seat and Park.
42. *Astragalus Hypoglottis* L., Purple Milk-vetch. Queen's Park; very pretty in early summer.
43. *Lathyrus pratensis* L., Yellow Meadow Vetchling. Hedges about Duddingston.

NATURAL ORDER **Rosaceæ**—Rose Family.

44. *Spiræa Filipendula* L., Common Dropwort. Queen's Park, not now common.
45. *Alchemilla vulgaris* L., Common Lady's Mantle. Queen's Park, common.

46. *Potentilla verna* L., Spring Cinquefoil. South side of Park, dry places; one of our rarer spring flowers.
47. *Potentilla reptans* L., Creeping Cinquefoil. Craigmillar, not plentiful.
48. *Rubus Idæus* L., Common Raspberry. East side of Arthur's Seat.
49. *Rosa spinosissima* L., Burnet-leaved Rose. Still to be found in Queen's Park.

NATURAL ORDER **Onagrarieæ**—Evening Primrose Family.

50. *Epilobium palustre* L., Narrow-leaved Marsh Willow-herb. Side of loch.
51. *Epilobium parviflorum* Schreb., Small-flowered Hairy Willow-herb. Side of loch.
52. *Epilobium hirsutum* L., Great Hairy Willow-herb. Side of loch.

NATURAL ORDER **Halorageæ**—Mare's-tail Family.

53. *Hippuris vulgaris* L., Common Mare's-tail. Duddingston Loch.

NATURAL ORDER **Crassulaceæ**—Stonecrop Family.

54. *Sedum acre* L., Biting Stonecrop. South side of Park, in rocky places.
55. *Saxifraga granulata* L., White Meadow Saxifrage. North side of loch, on dry ground.

NATURAL ORDER **Umbelliferæ**—Umbelliferous Family.

56. *Hydrocotyle vulgaris* L., Marsh Penny-wort. West side of loch, on boggy ground.
57. *Helosciadium nodiflorum* Koch., Procumbent Marshwort. East side of loch, not very abundant.

58. *Helosciadium nodiflorum* var. *repens*, Creeping Marshwort. East side of loch; not a common plant in the British flora.
59. *Ægopodium Podagraria* L., Common Gout-weed. Craigmillar, plentiful.
60. *Bunium flexuosum* With., Common Earth-nut. Queen's Park, plentiful.
61. *Sium angustifolium* L., Narrow-leaved Water-parsnip. Margin of loch, plentiful; not often found in Scotland.
62. *Torilis nodosa* Gaert., Hedgehog Parsley. Queen's Park, in dry places.
63. *Myrrhis odorata* Scop., Sweet Cicely. Craigmillar.
64. *Smyrnium Olusatrum* L., Common Alexanders. Craigmillar.

NATURAL ORDER **Rubiaceæ**—Madder Family.

65. *Galium palustre* L., White Water Bed-straw. Margin of loch.
66. *Sherardia arvensis* L., Blue Sherardia or Field-Madder. South side of Park, not plentiful; apt to be overlooked from its diminutive size.

NATURAL ORDER **Compositæ**—Composite Family.

67. *Filago germanica* L., Cudweed. South side of Park, on dry sandy places.
68. *Senecio aquaticus* Huds., Marsh Ragwort. Margin of loch, common.
69. *Senecio viscosus* L., Stinking Groundsel. Not a common plant generally, but very plentiful on Arthur's Seat.
70. *Lapsana communis* L., Common Nipplewort. Queen's Park and Craigmillar.
71. *Sonchus asper* Hoffm., Sharp-fringed Annual Sow-thistle. South side of Park, not plentiful.

72. *Crepis virens* L., Smooth Hawk's Beard. South side of Park, common.
73. *Hieracium Pilosella* L., Mouse-ear Hawk-weed. Queen's Park and Duddingston, common.

NATURAL ORDER **Gentianeæ**—Gentian Family.

74. *Menyanthes trifoliata* L., Buckbean or Bogbean. South side of loch.

NATURAL ORDER **Boragineæ**—Borage Family.

75. *Anchusa sempervirens* L., Evergreen Alkanet. South side of Craigmillar Castle, not plentiful.
76. *Symphytum officinale* L., Common Comfrey. Craigmillar.
77. *Echium vulgare* L., Common Viper's Bugloss. North slope of Arthur's Seat, abundant; sparingly on south side.
78. *Myosotis palustris* With., Water Scorpion-Grass. Margin of loch, common in spring.
79. *Myosotis arvensis* Hoffm., Field Scorpion-Grass. South side of Park.

NATURAL ORDER **Scrophularineæ**—Figwort Family.

80. *Veronica scutellata* L., Marsh Speedwell. Margin of loch.
81. *Veronica Anagallis* L., Water Speedwell. Margin of loch.
82. *Veronica Beccabunga* L., Brooklime. Margin of loch.

NATURAL ORDER **Labiatæ**—Deadnettle Family.

83. *Mentha aquatica* L., Water Capitate Mint. Margin of loch.
84. *Lamium amplexicaule* L., Henbit Deadnettle. Hedge-bank at Duddingston.
85. *Lamium incisum* Willd., Cut-leaved Deadnettle. Hedge-bank at Duddingston.

NATURAL ORDER **Chenopodiaceæ**—Goosefoot Family.

86. *Chenopodium Bonus-Henricus* L., Good King Henry or Mercury Goosefoot. Craigmillar.

NATURAL ORDER **Polygoneæ**—Buckwheat Family.

87. *Rumex conglomeratus* Murr., Sharp Dock. Margin of loch, common.
88. *Polygonum amphibium* L., Amphibious Buckwheat. Abundant in loch, both in shallow and deep water.

NATURAL ORDER **Irideæ**—Iris Family.

89. *Iris Pseud-acorus* L., Yellow Water Iris. Margin of loch.

NATURAL ORDER **Junceæ**—Rush Family.

90. *Juncus effusus* L., Common Soft Rush. Queen's Park and Duddingston.
91. *Juncus bufonius* L., Toad Rush. Margin of loch.

NATURAL ORDER **Alismaceæ**—Water-Plantain Family.

92. *Alisma Plantago* L., Greater Water-Plantain. Shallow and deep water in loch, plentiful.
93. *Butomus umbellatus* L., Flowering Rush. Duddingston Loch, not plentiful.

NATURAL ORDER **Typhaceæ**—Bulrush Family.

94. *Sparganium ramosum* Huds., Branched Bur-reed. East end of loch, plentiful.

NATURAL ORDER **Cyperaceæ**—Sedge Family.

95. *Eleocharis palustris* Br., Creeping Spike-rush. Duddingston Loch, and wet places in Queen's Park.

96. *Carex ovalis* Good., Oval-spiked Carex. Margin of loch.
97. *Carex riparia* Curt., Great Common Carex. Margin of loch.

NATURAL ORDER **Filices**—Fern Family.

98. *Asplenium septentrionale* Hull, Forked Spleenwort. Arthur's Seat and Samson's Ribs, not now plentiful.
99. *Asplenium Ruta-muraria* L., Wall-Rue. Abundant on old walls about Queen's Park and Duddingston.

NATURAL ORDER **Equisetaceæ**—Horse-tail Family.

100. *Equisetum palustre* L., Marsh Horse-tail. Margin of loch, common.

[Grasses and Mosses, not included in the above list, are rather plentiful in the district. About forty species of Grasses and over twenty species of Mosses are given for this comparatively small area in Balfour's 'Flora of Edinburgh,' though some of these are no longer to be found there.]

VI.

The Geological Features.

The Craigmillar district has long been held to be one of the most favoured spots in Scotland, from a geologist's point of view. Few places, indeed, offer to the geologist so many advantages, and afford such a varied field for his investigations. Within a radius of a few miles from Craigmillar Castle a section of the earth's crust can be had embracing a series of rock groups from the Lower Silurian to the upper members of the Carboniferous System. It will thus be evident that before we could have such a rich field of observation laid out before us, within so limited an area, the various agencies that have contributed to bring about such remarkable results must necessarily have been of a gigantic kind. The neighbourhood furnishes numerous examples of the violent nature of these agencies, and the part they played in the configuration of the surrounding country as we now see it.

The greater part of the South of Scotland belongs to the Lower Silurian system, the earlier beds of this series of rocks forming the range of the Moorfoot Hills, which border the southern extremity of the region we propose including in our sketch of the geology of the Craigmillar district. This system may be fairly taken as representing the backbone on which the upper groups of later deposits rest; and from these beds of the Lower Silurian we will ask the reader to accompany us while we endeavour to explain the different and successive measures as they occur—taking them up, as far as possible, in their geological sequence.

Following this range in a westerly direction, the Lower Silurian of the Moorfoots abuts against the Pentlands, giving place to the upper members of the same system, these again being surmounted by the sandstones and grits of the Old Red Sandstone forming this part of the Pentlands. The Pentlands themselves, stretching in a north-easterly direction towards the south of Edinburgh, are joined at their northern end by the Braid and Blackford hills. The Pentlands attain a considerable elevation, some parts being fully 1900 feet above sea-level. This range of hills plays a very important part in the stratification of the district, forming a great anticline, with its axis extending along the line of the ridge, and continuing northwards till it reaches the sea,—its effect on the strata being to alter the bedding, and cause it to dip in an easterly and westerly direction from its sides. On the east side of the anticline this alteration of the strata is much augmented by a great fault or dislocation which runs along the base and parallel with the Pentlands, throwing up the lower beds of the Calciferous Sandstone series—*i.e.*, the red-coloured sandstones that rest on the top of the Old Red Sandstone.

The Carboniferous or coal-bearing rocks of Scotland have been divided into four groups—namely: (1) The Calciferous Sandstone series, which occupy the lowest position; (2) The Carboniferous Limestone series; (3) The Millstone Grit series; and (4) The Upper or Flat Coal-measures.

Each of these groups is well represented in the neighbourhood of Craigmillar. Beginning with the lowest of them, we have already seen how the strata of the first or Calciferous Sandstone series have been folded over the Pentland anticline, and the lower beds of the same formation tilted up by the great fault on the east side, so that instead of having the same strata appearing on both sides of the anticline, those on the east side are of a much earlier date. This formation extends in a narrow belt or strip along the foot of the Pentlands on its eastern side as far as Carlops, running along the base of the Moorfoots, and turning northwards by Borthwick and Roman Camp, eventually reaching the sea at Aberlady, and forming the outer edge of the Mid-Lothian coal-basin. To the west of Edinburgh, and west of the Pentland anticline, the strata of this formation are more fully represented than on the east side, the Pentland fault having thrown out a considerable depth of strata in the latter, so that we have the Burdiehouse Limestone, with a comparatively thin section of strata intervening between it and the Gilmerton Limestone (the lower limestone of the next series above), where, on the other hand, upwards of 2500 feet of strata occur between the two limestones on the west side. The oil-shales, so extensively worked in Mid-Lothian and Linlithgowshire, belong principally to this division of the Calciferous Sandstone group, namely, between the two limestones of Burdiehouse and Gilmerton. The Carboniferous Limestone series—the next division following the Calciferous Sandstone—begins in the district with the Gilmerton Limestone — the bottom limestone of the group. Above this other two limestones occur; following these, a series of sandstones, with several workable seams of coal; then an ironstone; and above these again, other bands of limestone, forming the top of the group. The coals and ironstones are extensively worked in the neighbourhood of Loanhead, Gilmerton, and Niddrie. Owing to the Pentland fault, the strata adjoining it are highly inclined, and are known locally as the " edge coals "; above these comes the third group of strata, known as the Millstone Grit; and finally, on the top of the Millstone Grit, the last division of the Carboniferous System—the Flat or true Coal-measures of the Dalkeith coal-field.

These four groups, as we have them east of Craigmillar, form an immense basin, the northern side of which is cut off by the sea. On the opposite or Fife shore the strata again appear, and much in the same order. Above the Carboniferous system no rocks of a later date occur in the district—nothing, in fact, till the deposits of the Glacial Period, namely, boulder-clay and drift accumulations.

The Igneous Rocks of the district present a very striking appearance in the landscape—Arthur's Seat, a volcanic neck, with the basalt plug forming its apex, probably of early Carboniferous age; and the high mural escarpment of Salisbury Crags, consisting of dolerite ejected between strata of the Calciferous Sandstone. This bed, as well as that known as the St Leonard's Crag, were both ejected late in the geological scale, and belong to Tertiary times. These bold escarpments afford most important evidence of the denudation of the district, with the characteristic "crag-and-tail" of the different prominences, such as the Castle Rock of Edinburgh, the Calton Hill, and Salisbury Crags. The igneous rocks of the Pentlands very probably had their origin during Old

Red Sandstone times; while there can be no doubt that the porphyrites and felstones of the northern end of the range were erupted during the close of the deposition of the upper beds of the Old Red Sandstone and the beginning of the Carboniferous system. The Mid-Lothian basin is comparatively free from eruptive rocks, with the exception of a dyke that cuts through the most northerly part of the basin, and which, probably, is a continuation to the east of one of the parallel dykes which traverse the midland counties of Scotland west of Edinburgh.

The environs of Craigmillar and the adjacent district afford ample scope to the collector of fossils, nearly all the rocks we have mentioned being fossiliferous. The beds of the Lower Silurian system are but sparingly fossiliferous, although they offer a good field for the geologist, and will repay the labour of those disposed to devote their time to this series of strata. The Upper Silurian of the Pentlands has yielded a goodly number of fossils. Some fossiliferous beds of this formation occur at Nine-Mile-Burn, on the Pentlands, south-west of Glencorse. The Old Red Sandstone of the Pentlands, so far as known, is not fossiliferous. The Carboniferous rocks of the neighbourhood are everywhere rich in fossil remains,

SCALE OF FISH (*Rhizodus Hibbertii*), Burdiehouse.
(*Nat. size—Carboniferous.*)

which are easily got at. The Burdiehouse Limestone, a calciferous limestone, has long been a favourite hunting-ground for Edinburgh geologists. The limestone, being of an estuarine nature, contains many beautiful specimens of fish teeth, scales, &c., besides

PORTION OF JAW OF FISH (*Rhizodus Hibbertii*), Gilmerton.
(*Half nat. size—Carboniferous.*)

furnishing numerous fine forms of plant life, as ferns,

lepidodendra, stigmaria, &c. The Gilmerton Limestone, being higher in the scale, and a marine deposit, furnishes many good specimens of corals, encrinites, and shells. The coal workings in this group of strata at Loanhead, Gilmerton, and Niddrie are all favourable places for the collector. The belt of strata known as the Millstone Grit is, comparatively speaking, unfossiliferous, few specimens being found in any of the beds, and those which are present being probably stragglers from the formation below. The Upper Coal-measures of the Dalkeith coal-field are, however, rich in fossil remains, and from the number of pits, and the refuse-heaps of disused workings in this group, many opportunities of securing specimens are offered to the collector.

Those interested in the action of ice during the Glacial Period will find numerous examples of glaciation in the neighbourhood. Scarcely a projecting rock, indeed, but shows unmistakable evidence of the polishing it has undergone, the striæ, in many cases, being very fine. Good examples of this glacial action are to be seen at Arthur's Seat, the top of Salisbury Crags, and the Queen's Drive above Samson's Ribs, as well as along the ridge of the Pentlands. At the south-west side of Arthur's Seat, where the Queen's Drive passes between the main body of the hill and the knoll above Samson's Ribs, some beautiful examples of ice-worn rocks were exposed to view

ICE-WORN SURFACE OF ROCK, QUEEN'S DRIVE
(South-west side of Arthur's Seat).

during the construction of the roadway, part of which can now be seen, on the left side of the road going east, as shown in the above illustration.

The physical conditions of the district we have been viewing, as, indeed, of the whole of the northern hemisphere, during what is known as the Ice Age or Glacial Period, must have been simply marvellous, taxing the powers of the human imagination to conceive of them. According to Sir Archibald Geikie, "the high grounds of Britain were important enough to have their own independent ice, which, as the striæ show, radiated outward, some of it passing westwards into the Atlantic, and some of it eastward into the North Sea." The mass of ice which thus moved over Scotland, and south as far as Middlesex, at that period was so great that the broad plains of Perthshire are believed to have been filled up by it to a depth of fully 2000 feet. The subject is too wide and technical for any extended notice in a work such as the present; but there is now an extensive literature upon it, notably Professor J. Geikie's classical work, 'The Great Ice Age.' Several local geologists, also, have described the glacial features of the Edinburgh district, where, as we have already remarked, examples of ice-action are numerous. The "deposits" of the Glacial Period—the boulder-clay and drift—already mentioned, are also numerous and well marked in this district. Indeed, the greater part of the New

Town of Edinburgh is built on the boulder-clay. Several examples of the huge blocks of stone, or "travelled rocks," characteristic of the boulder-clay deposit, are found in this neighbourhood, more particularly at the sea-shore, where they have often proved a source of wonder to observers not acquainted with their history. The boulder-clays, as well as the whole subject of the natural features of this district during successive geological periods, were described by the late Hugh Miller, in his well-known picturesque style, in two lectures delivered to the members of the Edinburgh Philosophical Institution. These lectures are now included in a posthumous volume entitled 'Edinburgh and its Neighbourhood.'

Before concluding this short sketch of the geological features of the Craigmillar district, a few words may be said regarding the Craigmillar building-stone. Craigmillar sandstone has been quarried for centuries—the castle and other buildings in the district, including the older portion of The Inch House, having been built from it. In the erection of George Square, the Regent Bridge, the barracks at Piershill, the Edinburgh Water Company's reservoirs, and many edifices in the New Town, Craigmillar stone was used. In this age of haste and competition the stone is regarded as being too hard for architectural purposes; indeed, few smiths can now temper tools to withstand its adamantine nature. It is, however, unequalled for the building of dwelling-houses, being almost impervious to damp, a block of stone weighing practically no heavier after being steeped for days in water than it did when dry. It is also very useful for dock purposes, in consequence of its power of resistance to the action of salt water, and large contracts for its use have from time to time been entered into when harbours were about to be constructed. In the 'History of George Heriot's Hospital,' by William Steven, we are informed that, in the erection of that edifice, part of the material was brought from Craigmillar quarry. What is more remarkable is, that the stones were drawn in "cairts" by "wemen." "It must not be supposed," says the above-named writer, "that females were generally put to such servile and shocking work in the seventeenth century. . . . These women were hardened offenders, upon whom every kind of Church censure had been fruitlessly expended." In those days there were no houses of correction, and the magistrates apparently tried the effect of public exposure. To prevent the prisoners' escape locks and shackles were used, and men to watch over them.

There are several disused quarries around Craigmillar, some of which have been filled up with refuse from the city. To the north-west, but in close proximity to the castle, are two large excavations from which stones for the building of the docks at Leith were taken,—a line of railway running into both, and the rails being lifted at the termination of the contract. One of the quarries is still worked; while in the case of the other, buildings have been erected in it for the manufacture of rockets. That well-known writer, Dr Robert Chambers, in his 'Picture of Scotland,' says: "There is a popular tradition that the stone used in the earliest construction of Edinburgh Castle was taken from Craigmillar. It is still further affirmed that it was built by the Picts, and that, in the want of wheeled carriages, these indefatigable artificers—who, by the way, get the credit in Scotland of building all old or stupendous public works—transported the stone in their hands, a line of carriers being planted all the way between the quarry and the castle, and each individual handing the huge lump forward to his next neighbour, who in his turn sent it still farther on towards its destination." If the Picts, unlike the builders of the Pyramids, possessed no mechanical contrivances, the labour of transporting blocks of stone by hand from Craigmillar quarry to the top of the Castle rock at Edinburgh, must have been great indeed!

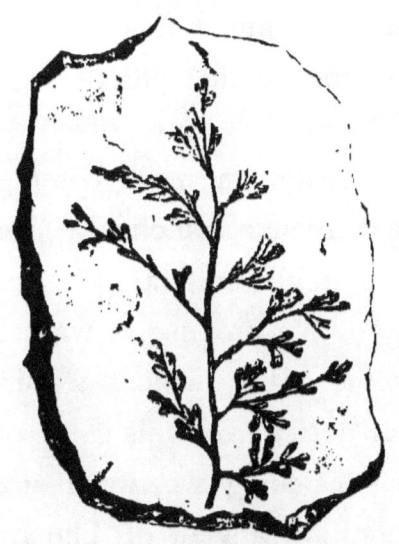

CARBONIFEROUS FERN
(*Sphenopteris affinis*), Burdiehouse   (*Nat. size.*)

VII.

The Environs of Craigmillar.

As indicated in a previous chapter, a magnificent panorama meets the gaze of the observer from the battlements of Craigmillar Castle. Dr Begg, in his Statistical Account of the parish in 1839, says of the castle: "It is the heart of Mid-Lothian, and there is not in Britain a more commanding view of rich and varied scenery, including wood, water, a fine city, and a richly cultivated country, than may be got from it." We propose in what follows to take up in order some of the salient features which thus come under our notice from this coign of vantage.

THE INCH.—Looking westward from the battlements of Craigmillar, a view of The Inch House can be obtained, peeping out from amongst the trees.

"Inch," as is well known, signifies an island, and at one time the house was surrounded by water, the

THE INCH HOUSE AS IT WAS.

access to it being by means of a drawbridge. Even within recent years, after exceptionally heavy rains the surrounding parks have been so extensively inundated as to resemble a lake. From a charter granted in the fourteenth century, The Inch appears to have belonged to the Abbey of Holyrood. The oldest date on the house is 1617, above a doorway, which was the original and only entrance at that period. The date 1634 also appears above a window on the lower part of the house, indicating that it must have been an addition. The initials of Winram, descended from the Winrams of Clydesdale, show that it belonged to that family. Besides The Inch, they were possessors of Nether Liberton and part of Over Liberton. The right of the north aisle in the kirk was ratified to Winrame of Liberton in 1621.[1] George Winram of Liberton, son of James Winram of Liberton, was admitted advocate on 20th December 1626. He undertook in 1639 the somewhat dangerous task of presenting to the king, at London, the Act of the General Assembly which abolished Episcopacy, to which the king replied, " When they have broken my head they will put

[1] 'Index to Scottish Acts of Parliament,' p. 779.

Inch House.

on my cowl." Mr Winram did considerable service to the cause of the Covenant during his residence in England. He was one of the Commissioners for the county of Edinburgh in the Parliaments of 1643 and 1649, and a member of the various committees of estate and war which were formed from time to time. He was appointed colonel of one of the regiments in the army ordered to be raised for the defence of the country in February 1649, and in the following month was sent by the General Assembly to accompany the Commissioners from the Estates appointed to treat with Charles II., then in Holland, as to the terms on which he could be allowed to assume the government of Scotland. Mr Winram was a second time sent, in November 1649, as the bearer of a letter from the Estates urging Charles to comply with their requests. He was admitted as an Ordinary Lord, under the title of Lord Liberton, on 22d June 1649, immediately after his first return from the Continent.

Lord Liberton took part in the Battle of Dunbar on September 3, 1650, and was so severely wounded that he died eight days afterwards. August 1650 must have been an exciting time for the inhabitants of Craigmillar and its environs. Cromwell is beleaguering the city. General Leslie has it strongly defended—his troops and cannon situated on the Calton Hill, Arthur's Seat, and Salisbury Crags. Cromwell successively occupies Musselburgh, Niddrie, the Braids, and the Pentlands. Skirmishes occur every day. Parleys, too, are frequently held on Bruntsfield Links and the Boroughmoor, with no satisfactory result. To Cromwell's disgust, cautious David Leslie is not to be drawn from his strong position. The castle defends the west side of the city. Eventually Cromwell has to fall back on Dunbar for supplies. Before he has passed Niddrie, General Leslie's cannon is hurrying his march by thundering away from the heights of Craigmillar. After the battle, Cromwell, in his brief despatches to the Speaker of the English Parliament, dated

4th September 1650, says: "What officers of theirs of quality are killed we cannot yet learn, but surely divers are; and many men of quality are mortally wounded, as Colonel Lumsden, the Lord Liberton, and others." In The Inch House is carefully treasured a sword which is said to have belonged to Oliver Cromwell. An inscription on the blade records the following: " Belonged to Oliver Cromwell, Lord Protector, Naseby Battle, June 14, 1646; Dunbar Battle, September 3, 1650. Praise to the Lord of Hosts."

The Inch was acquired by the Gilmours about the same time that they bought Craigmillar, but when they came to reside there does not appear to be recorded. Various additions were made to the house at the beginning of this century, but the present proprietor demolished the greater part of these, and reconstructed it in the old baronial style, in 1891-92.

Up till very recently there stood at the side of the western avenue of The Inch a group of picturesque old thatched cottages, which formed the subject of many an artist's canvas. These cottages were a remnant of the village of Nether Liberton. This village stood on both sides of the Braid Burn, and, like many other villages, contained a cross, all traces of which have long since disappeared. Formerly the village was of considerable size, as in 1786 it con-

OLD COTTAGES AT THE INCH.

tained nearly three hundred inhabitants. The mill at Nether Liberton is of great antiquity, it being on record that the " soir sanct," David I., bestowed it upon the monks of Holyrood, as a tithe thereof, with thirty cart-loads from the bush of Liberton;

and that Robert the Bruce, in 1326, granted to the monastery of the Blackfriars in Edinburgh six merks, and enjoined them to be paid out of his mill at Nether Liberton.

Close to the western entrance to The Inch stands a large dovecot, indicative of proximity to the resi-

DOVECOT AND MILL-DAM, NETHER LIBERTON.

dence of the Lord of the Barony. About three hundred years ago no one was allowed to erect a dovecot except owners of land. Thus, on the 28th of June 1617 an Act of Parliament was passed ordaining that no person should have power, liberty, or privilege to build a dovecot upon any lands except those who have lands and teinds pertaining to him, extending in yearly rent to ten chalders victual adjacent to the said dovecot, and one dovecot only to be built within said bounds.

"Good's Corner," Nether Liberton.

Stringent Acts were also passed against breakers, destroyers, and robbers of dovecots. The dovecot above referred to stands by the side of a dam for storing water to supply the ancient mill of Nether Liberton with water-power.

To the west of Nether Liberton is the Borough-moor of old, where the forces of Edward III., led by Guy, Count of Namure, were routed by the Scotch under the Earl of Murray and William de Douglas in 1336; and also where James IV. reviewed his troops prior to his departure for the fatal field of Flodden; but which bids fair at no distant date to be covered by houses, a large portion of it being already built upon. West from Nether Liberton may be seen the red sandstone gateway which commemorates the achievement of the Lord Provost of that date, Sir George Harrison, of acquiring in 1884, as a public park for the citizens of Edinburgh, the Blackford Hill, so indissolubly associated with Sir Walter Scott's "Marmion," as in the following lines:—

> "Suffice it that the route was laid
> Across the furzy hills of Braid.
> They passed the glen and scanty rill,
> And climbed the opposing bank, until
> They gained the top of Blackford Hill."

A site has been chosen on Blackford Hill for the erection of a National Scottish Observatory. This building, with its magnificent telescope from Dunecht and other astronomical and electrical instruments, bequeathed to Government for this purpose by the late Earl of Crawford and Balcarres, has been designed by Mr W. W. Robertson, of H.M.'s Board of Works, and will be one of the finest and most complete erections of the kind in the country.

LIBERTON.—To the south lie Liberton village, Upper Liberton, Liberton House, and Liberton Tower, which were all included in the barony of Over Liberton, and are interesting in their historical associations. We shall take up these parts of the ancient barony in their order; and first, of the village itself. Seen from afar, on the crown of the hill, is the handsome parish church of Liberton, re-erected in 1815. There are records of Liberton still extant which date back to the days of David I., some of these being witnessed by a Baron of Liberton named Macbeth. In the village stands the old schoolmaster's house, the supposed residence of Reuben Butler in Sir Walter Scott's 'Heart of Mid-Lothian.' Well into the present century, and within the memory of persons still living, on Fastern's-e'en the school at Liberton was for the nonce converted into a cockpit. Every boy in the advanced classes was expected to furnish a bird to take part in this cruel pastime. The first prize was a Bible, and the second a Testament! The birds killed in the fight became the

LIBERTON FROM THE BOROUGHMOOR.

perquisite of the schoolmaster. It seems scarcely credible that such a comparatively short time only should have elapsed since these barbarous practices prevailed. It may be remembered that Hugh Miller, in his charming autobiographical work, 'My Schools and Schoolmasters,' gives a graphic account of similar scenes in his boyhood. It is certainly matter for thankfulness that nowadays such "sport" is confined to the lowest stratum of society, and that amongst our youth the cock-fights, which were annual events

LIBERTON INDUSTRIAL SCHOOL.

in most of the parochial schools in Scotland, have given place to healthy athletic sports.

On the south side of the village stands the Industrial School. Nearly a century has elapsed since John Pounds, the poor cobbler of Portsmouth, put into execution the novel idea of collecting the street arabs into his little workroom, sometimes holding out the bait of a roasted potato to induce them to enter, with the view of teaching them to read. It was a print hanging in a village inn, representing this cobbler's room, and John Pounds sitting with an old shoe between his knees, looking over his spectacles on a number of ragged boys and girls who stood round him with lesson-book in hand, that first aroused the interest of Dr Guthrie, and stirred him up to take such a prominent part in the work of ragged-schools. That far-seeing Scottish clergyman realised the truth of the adage that "prevention is better than cure," and that a small expenditure on schools was a wiser investment than spending large sums on jails. An association was therefore formed to reclaim the children of the lapsed masses, and endeavour to check crime at the fountain-head by giving such children the benefits of education, and training them to habits of industry. It is now nearly half-a-century since the Industrial School was instituted at the Castlehill, in Edinburgh;

and in 1887 the building at Liberton was opened by the present Earl of Hopetoun, when Lord High Commissioner to the General Assembly of the Church of Scotland. Not only do the children here receive moral and religious teaching, but when aptitude for any special trade or profession is displayed, it receives the fullest encouragement. An efficient music-teacher and band-master are kept; and a brass band, and also a band of pipers, are trained in the establishment—their services at public entertainments being in frequent demand, both in England and Scotland.

Proceeding now to speak shortly of UPPER LIBERTON, it would be superfluous to trace all the proprietors of the barony, which appears frequently to have changed hands, and goes back to an early date. In the 'Register of the Great Seal' it is stated that on 8th March 1475 the king concedes to Alexander Dalmahoy the lands of the Barony of Uvir Libertoune. The Dalmahoys of that ilk possessed Upper Liberton as early as the year 1453, and continued in possession of it, or at least a part of it, for almost two hundred years. We

LIBERTON INDUSTRIAL SCHOOL PIPERS.

also learn from writings in the custody of the present laird that Robert Dalmahoy, with consent of his wife, Janet Robertson, granted a charter of certain lands in Upper Liberton to Thomas Levyntoune, burgess in Edinburgh, dated August 13, 1455. Again quoting from the 'Register of the Great Seal,' it is stated that on 4th May 1536 the king confirms the charter of Henry Cant of Over Liberton to Henry Creighton of Riccarton of the superiority of the mansion, tower, and fortalice of Over Liberton, with houses and gardens, vulgarly called "the Serjandis land." These lands lie to the south of the road leading to Blackford quarry. A charter of them was granted by King David II. to David Libbertoun, along with the office of "Sergandrie of the overward of the constabularie of Edinburgh."

The Dalmahoys, it appears, retained a portion of the barony, as we find by a charter dated 15th July 1528 that Alexander Dalmahoy of that ilk granted to Clement Little, burgess of Edinburgh, and Elizabeth Fisher, his spouse, a merk land of the two-merk lands called Rinzeanis, on the resignation of Henry Cant of Over Liberton. This Clement was father of Mr Clement Little, advocate, and William Little, merchant in, and Provost of, Edinburgh. The Littles were men of great influence, were much esteemed in Edinburgh, and at length became proprietors of the whole barony of Upper Liberton, which is still held intact by their direct descendant, Captain Gordon Gilmour. Clement Little in 1563 was appointed a Commissioner for trial of ecclesiastical complaints in Edinburgh, and in 1567 was one of three appointed procurators to defend, and pursue, all actions pertaining to the Kirk.[1] In the 'History of the University of Edinburgh' it is stated that Clement Little, advocate, and one of the Commissioners of Edinburgh, bequeathed his books on Theology and Law to that university. The Town Council accepted this gift, and on 14th October 1580 the books were presented by William Little, each volume being stamped with the arms of his brother, and with the words, "I am gevin to Edinburgh and kirk of God be Maister Clement Litil,

[1] Calderwood's 'History.'

thar to remain, 1580." These books are still in good preservation. In Pitcairn's 'Criminal Trials' (p. 261) it is stated that William Little, Provost of Edinburgh, was on commission for examining witches in 1587.

On 2d June 1592 Mr Walter Balcanquall, in his sermon, charged the king and nobility with great negligence of their duties. The king requested the Lords of the Articles to agree to an Act against such liberty of speech, and to a commission to some special magistrates to pull the ministers out of the pulpit when they spoke after that manner. He directed his speech specially to William Little, who was then Provost. Mr Little, however, replied, "Sir, you may discharge me of my office if you please, but that I cannot do." "What!" said the king; "will you prefer them to me?" "I will prefer God before man," said the Provost. On the 17th December 1596 William Little, along with Walter Balcanquall and other nine persons, were apprehended for "the treasonable and seditious stirring up and moving of the treasonable tumult and uproar that was in the Burgh of Edinburgh," and were lodged in the Castle.

William, the Provost, had two sons, Clement and William. Clement died without issue, and William became proprietor. He was succeeded by his son, also William, who acquired the entire barony by a purchase from Mr George Winram in 1641. The barony of Liberton appears to have previously been equally divided between them, as at the valuation of the teinds in 1630, exactly the same number of bolls of victual were assigned to each proprietor. He died in 1662, and was succeeded by his son, William, whose wife strongly favoured the Covenanters. In Fountainhall's 'Historical Notices' (p. 664) it is stated that on 25th May 1685 Little of Liberton's lady was one of the martyrs during the persecution. She was imprisoned for harbouring conventiclers, but on his entering prison for her, she was liberated.

It was in the time of this proprietor, William Little, that the present LIBERTON HOUSE was built, in 1675. This edifice has from time to time been modernised, by which "improvements" its steeply pitched roof was destroyed, and its crow-stepped gables were hidden beneath a mass of superincumbent masonry. It still presents, with but slight change, the usual characteristics of the "single" house of the 17th century—a type of building of which the author of 'The Heart of Mid-Lothian' speaks somewhat disparagingly. Owing to its sequestered situation and apparently uneventful history, Liberton House is still comparatively unknown. Until quite recently, even those who lived under its roof had no suspicion of the many features of interest that lay concealed under modern plaster

PEEP OF LIBERTON HOUSE.

and woodwork. These features, with the hearty approval and co-operation of the proprietor, have been gradually brought to light by the present tenant, Mr Godfrey G. Cunninghame, and the house now appears much as it may have done in its palmy days, while still the country residence of the family who owned it. Very interesting to the antiquarian are the great fireplaces, as well as the " squints," " shutter-board " windows, and other curious arrangements for defence or for guarding against sudden surprise—the latter especially being a very necessary provision in those troublous times. The doorways, framed in hammer-nigged stone of the hardest grain, and the quaint specimens of iron-work, are all preserved in their ancient form, visibly connecting the present with the past. The illustration presents one of the salient features of the western elevation, a rectangular turret boldly corbelled out from the circular staircase which it surmounts, and terminating in a crow-stepped gable of acute pitch.

William Little, who built Liberton House, had no family, and when he died in 1686 the estate was

WM. CHARLES LITTLE OF LIBERTON.

entailed upon his nephew, William Rankine, who assumed the name of Little, and married Helen, daughter of Sir Alexander Gilmour of Craigmillar, by whom he had only one child, Grizel. Dying in 1714, he was succeeded by his eldest brother, Gabriel, as heir male; and he dying in 1737, was in turn succeeded by his son, Walter Little of Liberton, who married his cousin, Grizel Little, and died in 1758. His son, William Charles Little of Liberton, succeeded to the Craigmillar property on the death of Sir Alexander Gilmour in 1792, and took the name of Little Gilmour of Liberton and Craigmillar. William Charles Little was an advocate in Edinburgh, and a member of the Society of the Antiquaries of Scotland. He displayed considerable literary ability, and interesting contributions from his pen, including "A Historical Account of the Hammermen of Edinburgh from their Records," and "An Inquiry into the Expedients used by the Scots before the Discovery of Metals," are recorded in the 'Proceedings' of the Society referred to.

We have little or no record as to when LIBERTON

Tower was built, or by whom. Messrs M'Gibbon and Ross, in their valuable work on the 'Castellated and Domestic Architecture of Scotland,' state that it is a simple keep of the fifteenth century, though, from

LIBERTON TOWER.

the extreme plainness of its form, and its generally frail and dilapidated condition, it is frequently assigned to a much earlier period. The simple quadrilateral outline is quite usual, and the internal arrangements are somewhat similar to those of Lochleven Castle, associated with memories of Queen Mary. Liberton Tower is divided into two by a semicircular vault in the centre, above which is the hall. The ground-floor is very low in the roof, and has probably been used for sheltering cattle. It has now a separate outer door, but formerly had no communication except through the upper rooms by a hatch in the floor above. The upper portion is also vaulted with a pointed barrel vault, which carries the stone roof and battlements. Those who have visited the Tower will have noticed that there have been intermediate floors, the oak beams resting on corbels. The principal entrance to the Tower is on the level of the hall, on the east side of the building, fifteen feet from the ground, and must have been reached by a ladder. There is no properly formed stair to the parapet, which would no doubt be reached by a wooden stair inside, leading to the top door in the east gable. The inmates seem to have depended entirely on its strength for security, the parapet being carried up flush with the walls, and having no corbelling or machicolations through which stones or other missiles could be dropped upon assailants. The only thing in the shape of ornament in the Tower is the sideboard of the hall in the south wall, which has an ogee-headed opening, and is clearly indicative of the fifteenth century. As already noted,

VIEW FROM THE BRAIDS.

the Dalmahoys of that ilk possessed Over Liberton as early as 1453, and antiquarians are of opinion that the Tower was in all probability built by that family.

THE BRAIDS.—To the west of the Barony of Over

Liberton are the Braid Hills, covered on some parts by thick patches of whins. A portion of them was purchased by the city of Edinburgh in 1890 for a course on which the inhabitants might indulge in the game of golf. The southern part of the hill has also been leased from Colonel Trotter of Mortonhall for the same purpose by an Edinburgh club. The hill is even yet wild and romantic, and from the higher parts a magnificent and most extensive view can be obtained, of which no more graphic description could be given than that by Sir Walter Scott :—

> "But northward far, with purer blaze,
> On Ochil mountains fell the rays,
> And as each heathy top they kissed,
> It gleamed a purple amethyst.
> Yonder the shores of Fife you saw;
> Here Preston Bay and Berwick Law:
> And, broad between them rolled,
> The gallant Frith the eye might note,
> Whose islands on its bosom float,
> Like emeralds chased in gold."

In a hollow on the hill, at the march between the town property and that of Colonel Trotter, is a very pretty natural pond, much frequented at night by wild-fowl.

Another on the south side is called Elf's Kirk, denoting the place where the fairies assembled.

MORTONHALL.—To the south of the Braid Hills lies Mortonhall, already referred to. Situated in a hollow, it cannot be seen from a distance, but a little to the

MORTONHALL.

west is the elevated ground, now covered with wood, called Galach-law, famous for the encampment of Oliver Cromwell's army, which consisted of no less than 16,000 men. In the reign of James III. Mortonhall belonged to the St Clairs of Roslin, and came into possession of the ancestors of the present laird about 1641. The Trotters are an old family, dating back to the reigns of Robert II. and Robert III. of Scotland. The present branch is descended from Thomas Trotter, proprietor of the estates of Foulshaw, Catchelraw, and Kilnhill, in Berwickshire. The first Baron of Mortonhall was John Trotter, who was a stanch loyalist in the time of Charles II. He died in 1641, and was succeeded by his eldest son, John, who was also a steady loyalist, and was fined £500 sterling for assisting the Marquis of Montrose. After ten successive barons, the second son of the last one was Richard Trotter, who died in 1793, and was succeeded by his grandson, Richard Trotter, father of the present proprietor, Henry Trotter, Colonel of the Grenadier Guards.

THE BALM WELL.—At St Catherine's is still to be seen the famous "Balm well," which in bygone days of superstition was believed to possess a healing virtue for skin diseases. At the request of James VI. the well was in 1617 greatly adorned, a door and staircase made to it, and fenced with masonry from top to bottom. It was, however, completely wrecked by Cromwell's soldiers in 1650, and though afterwards restored, it never appeared again to the same advantage. A black oily substance floats on the surface of the well still, as it did of old, and is traceable to the exudation of the shale, which, as is well known, is abundant in the district.

BURDIEHOUSE and STRAITON.—Burdiehouse, it is asserted, is a corruption of "Bourdeaux" house, so called from some of the French retainers who came to Scotland with Queen Mary taking up their residence there. An abundance of limestone is found in the district, which is extensively worked by Sir David Baird, and with considerable success. As indicated in a previous chapter, there are found embedded in the limestone numerous specimens of plant and animal remains, which are extremely interesting to geologists. Straiton is one of those quiet uninteresting places through which the old coach-road to Penicuik, Peebles, and the South of Scotland passed. As the result of operations carried on by the Clippens and Straiton oil-companies, the amenity of the district has been literally destroyed and the social conditions of the locality entirely changed within the last quarter of a century, it being now the centre of a large mining population.

THE PENTLANDS.—The Pentland range, seen so conspicuously from Craigmillar, runs in a south-westerly direction into Peeblesshire. Its geological features have already been noticed in the chapter on that subject. The farthest point of the range within sight caps the undulating plain called Rullion Green, where the defeat of the Covenanters took place on 28th November 1666. The insurgents, led by Colonel James Wallace, were resting themselves as they best could, when suddenly they beheld General Dalziel's army approaching. The Royal troops were at once led to the assault. The Covenanters behaved with courage, and twice repulsed the attacks of the Royalists, but, as might be expected, nine hundred half-disciplined and ill-armed men could not cope with three thousand well-equipped soldiers led by an officer of Dalziel's experience. Fifty of the Covenanters were killed, and over a hundred made prisoners. The slain were buried at Rullion Green, an old monument still marking the spot. In 1858 the late Lord-President Inglis took steps to preserve this memorial, erected to the memory of the martyrs who fell in the Pentland Rising. On one side of it an inscription in rugged verse records—

> "A cloud of witnesses lie here,
> Who for Christ's interests did appear,
> For to restore true Liberty,
> O'erturned them by tyranny:
> These heroes fought with great renown;
> By falling got the martyr's crown!"

The reverse side of the monument appears as in the accompanying illustration. For a number of years an open-air religious service has been held annually at Rullion Green, large numbers from the surrounding district being often present. The scene on a summer Sabbath afternoon, in this retired historic spot, is peculiarly solemn and impressive, as the wail of some old Scottish psalm-tune rises into the still air, or the cadences of the preacher's voice die away among the surrounding hills. The mingled features of the land-

TOMBSTONE IN MEMORY OF THE COVENANTERS.

scape and the reverent congregation combine to make up just such a picture as the late Sir George Harvey would have loved to paint.

Among the most prominent of those who took part in the Pentland Rising was a young clergyman named Hugh M'Kail, son of Matthew M'Kail, the ousted minister of Bothwell. This young man was remarkable for his learning and impressive eloquence. In the last sermon he preached prior to the 8th September 1662, the day fixed by Parliament for the removal of the nonconforming ministers of the city, he referred to the persecution to which the Church was being subjected, remarking that the Church and people of God had been harassed by a Pharaoh upon the throne, a Haman in the State, and a Judas in the Church. For these remarks he was adjudged a traitor, and a party of dragoons was sent out to Moredun, near Liberton, a seat of Sir James Stewart's, to apprehend him; but he made his escape, and remained for a time in concealment in his father's house at Bothwell. In November 1666, as already said, he took a prominent part in the Pentland

Rising, but the day before the battle of Rullion Green he was in such a state of weakness and prostration that he was obliged to leave his comrades at Colinton. On his way to Liberton he was apprehended in passing over the Braid Hills, and committed prisoner to the Tolbooth of Edinburgh. After being subjected to that terrible instrument of torture, the "boot," in which his leg was shattered with eleven strokes of the mallet without extorting the sort of confession that was wanted, he was condemned for high treason, and hanged at the cross of Edinburgh. On the scaffold he spoke with such impressive eloquence to the vast assemblage, and with so rapturous a confidence of his future happiness, that there was scarcely a dry eye among the numerous spectators. At subsequent executions of the ringleaders amongst the Covenanters, the authorities caused drums to be beaten and trumpets to be sounded in order to drown the last words of these resolute men.

WOODHOUSELEE.—Near to Rullion Green is the site of Old Woodhouselee, which in 1570 belonged to Hamilton of Bothwellhaugh, in right of his wife.

The estate, however, had been confiscated, and part of it bestowed on Sir James Bellenden, Lord Justice-Clerk, who was a favourite of Regent Murray, then in power. Sir James seized upon the house, and turned out Hamilton's wife, with her infant child, in a cold November night, into the open fields, where before morning she became insane. Wounded to the quick by this inhuman act, Bothwellhaugh vowed to be revenged, resolving at last to wait till his enemy should pass through Linlithgow, on his way from Stirling to Edinburgh. Having secretly introduced himself, with his carbine, into an empty house favourable for his purpose, he barred the doors and windows looking to the street, and placed a fleet horse ready saddled at the back. Murray got a hint that danger lurked in this street, but considered it cowardly to turn, and kept on his way. Amid the vast assemblage he rode slowly past the fatal house, which gave Bothwellhaugh an opportunity for taking aim. He fired, and the Regent fell, mortally wounded. The soldiers rushed furiously at the door, but ere they could force an entrance Bothwellhaugh had escaped.

> " 'Mid pennoned spears, a steely grove,
>   Proud Murray's plumage floated high;
>   Scarce could his trampling charger move,
>   So close the minions crowded nigh.
>
> From the raised vizor's shade his eye,
>   Dark-rolling, glanced the ranks along;
>   And his steel truncheon, waved on high,
>   Seemed marshalling the iron throng.
>
> But yet his saddened brow confessed
>   A passing shade of doubt and awe;
>   Some fiend was whispering in his breast,
>   ' Beware of injured Bothwellhaugh!'
>
> The death-shot parts—the charger springs—
>   Wild rises tumult's startling roar,
>   And Murray's plumy helmet rings—
>   Rings on the ground, to rise no more."

The Sheriff-court offices now stand on the site of the house from which the Regent was shot, and a memorial tablet in bronze, designed by Sir Noël Paton, R.S.A., has been inserted into the building to mark the spot. This tablet contains a portrait of the Regent. The carbine—the barrel of which is of brass, and a small bore—is now in the possession of Lord Hamilton of Dalziel.

Several centuries have passed since old Woodhouselee ceased to be inhabited, although there are traditions of historic interest associated with it which still survive among the readers of Scottish story. Some of the stones from the ancient edifice were utilised in making additions to the present mansion-house of Woodhouselee, which was formerly known as the Tower of Fulford, and is about three miles distant from the ruins of old Woodhouselee. It is now the residence of James William Fraser-Tytler, Esq. Tradition asserts that both houses have been haunted by the ghost of Lady Bothwellhaugh, who appears customarily in white, and invariably carrying a child in her arms.

The Tytler family has produced several eminent men in their generation. Of these may be mentioned Lord Woodhouselee, one of the Senators of the College of Justice, who is still remembered as the author of the 'Life of Lord Kames' and other literary works; while his father, William Tytler, wrote a book of some importance in vindication of Queen Mary. The son of Lord Woodhouselee, again, Patrick Fraser - Tytler, advocate, was the author of the well-known and valuable 'History of Scotland' connected with his name. The late proprietor, James Stuart Fraser-Tytler, was for a number of years Professor of Conveyancing in the University of Edinburgh.

At Woodhouselee is to be seen a gold watch and jewelled solitaire which belonged to Queen Mary of Scots, and were given by her to Massi, a French attendant who followed her to Scotland. They were treasured by his descendants, and were for long the property of the family of Scott, chemists in Edinburgh, by the last of whom, Mrs Robert Scott, they were left to her brother, the Rev. William Torrance, minister of the parish of Glencorse. His son, the Rev. Alexander Torrance, bequeathed them to the late James Stuart Fraser-Tytler. In the year 1767, Lord Cardross, afterwards Earl of Buchan, borrowed them from Dr J. Scott, to take with him to the Conference in Spain. In a letter dated 1804,

SOLITAIRE.
(Worn by Queen Mary.)

Lord Buchan mentions that in an original portrait of Queen Mary in his possession, she is represented as wearing the solitaire.

The estate of Woodhouselee, it may be added, is very picturesque and interesting, and memories of Allan Ramsay and other celebrities of a bygone age still linger about its shady walks and retired nooks.

QUEEN MARY'S WATCH, AT WOODHOUSELEE.
(*Same size as original.*)

VIII.

Proximate Landscape.

In our concluding chapter we invite the reader once more to take a survey of the picturesque landscape from the battlements of the famous ruin. Immediately north of Craigmillar, and under the shadow of Arthur's Seat, lies the village of DUDDINGSTON, with its loch. It is recorded that large forests formerly existed near Duddingston, which afforded shelter to Sir William Wallace and his bold companions when on their way to attack Berwick. In the village may still be seen the house in which Prince Charlie slept the night before the battle of Prestonpans, in 1745. This house at that period belonged to Mr Horne, a farmer. For more than a month the Chevalier's forces were encamped by the brook side, in what is now known as the policies, both before and after he defeated General Cope. Duddingston at one time was owned by a family named Thomson, one of whom was made a baronet by Charles I. in 1637. It was acquired by the Duke of Lauderdale in 1674, and passed with his daughter to the first Duke of Argyle, to whom she was married. In 1745 it was sold to the Earl of Abercorn; and in 1768, the house, which is a beautiful specimen of Grecian architecture, was built, after a design by Sir William Chambers. The pleasure-grounds which surround it were also planned with great taste, and with the house cost £30,000. The late Mr Robert Forsyth described it as "an example of all that money or art can do to adorn a merely flat surface through which a small stream of water naturally runs; clumps, groves, canals, lakes, isles, cascades, shrubbery, serpentine walks, and spreading lawns. In every corner art and expense have been ostentatiously displayed, and nature is evidently employed merely as her handmaid." [1]

[1] 'Beauties of Scotland.'

At the base of Arthur's Seat is DUDDINGSTON LOCH, which, when frozen over, is largely taken advantage of by skaters. The dimensions of this lake have been curtailed through silting-up and the deepening of the outlet. It is supplied with water by springs from Arthur's Seat, and by a small stream from the west, which takes its rise in the "Wells o' Wearie," celebrated in song. It is certainly to be regretted that in these days of modern civilisation this beautiful sheet of water should be a receptacle for filthy sewage, so that fish life, with the exception of pike, perch, and eels, is thereby rendered impossible. Nowadays, when the memories of successive Lord Provosts are perpetuated by the acquisition of public parks, golf courses, and resorts for equestrian exercise for the citizens of Edinburgh, it is surprising that no one has suggested to clean out the loch, to divert the Pow or Braid burn into it, and to stock it with Loch Leven trout. From the number of disciples of Izaak Walton that may be seen on a summer evening, some of them standing to the knees in the mud, fishing for perch, it is safe to say that the

SKATERS ON DUDDINGSTON LOCH.

From a Photo by
JOHN PATRICK & SON, EDINBURGH

course indicated would to many be a great boon. Towards the close of the last century, in dredging the loch, the antlers of deer were discovered. There were also found some coins, the inscriptions on which were effaced, the blade of a sword, and the heads of some spears and javelins, all, from their structure and material, believed to be Roman. Some of these are now in the Antiquarian Museum in Edinburgh.

As mentioned in previous chapters, a large number of aquatic birds and marsh plants are present at Duddingston Loch; and the attention of entomologists is also periodically attracted by the variety of moths in its vicinity.

The parish church of Duddingston is of great antiquity, and is exceedingly interesting. At the gate is still to be seen the "jougs" hanging on the wall. In 1592 an Act of Parliament was passed that irons and stocks were to be provided at the parish kirks for punishing idle beggars and vagabonds.[1] Though long since fallen into disuse, the "jougs" are allowed to hang for the inspection of the curious, as a speci-

[1] Index to Scottish Acts of Parliament, p. 326.

men of the kind of punishment imposed in ruder times for petty offences.

On at least two occasions has the charge of Duddingston been held by remarkable ministers—the one in the domain of literature, and the other in that of art. The former, the Rev. Robert Monteith, an Episcopalian clergyman, had contracted an illicit amour with Lady Hamilton of Priestfield during her husband's absence. On the husband's return the rev. gentleman fled abroad, where he turned his attention to literature, and left behind him some interesting works written in the French language. The latter, the Rev. J. Thomson, was at the beginning of the present century regarded as one of the best landscape painters of his day. His paintings are of considerable value, some adorning the walls of the National Gallery in Edinburgh.

At some little distance from the village of Duddingston lies EASTER DUDDINGSTON, the most noteworthy feature of which is Easter Duddingston Lodge, with its beautiful grounds, the property of Charles Jenner, Esq. This house, before being remodelled by the present proprietor, was a very ancient structure, and evidences of its original strength are still visible in the back walls, which are of abnormal thickness. The grounds are a model of taste and skill, and contain specimens of rare trees, shrubs, and flowering-plants seldom met with in a private collection.

PEFFER MILL.—In close proximity to the south of Duddingston is Peffer Mill, the supposed residence of the Laird of Dumbiedykes, immortalised by Sir Walter Scott in 'The Heart of Mid-Lothian.' The house was built by one Edgar in 1636, and his arms, impaled with those of his wife, are still to be seen above the beautiful entrance-door. Below the arms are the mottoes, " Cui vult dat Deus ": "Dum spiro spero." "God gives to whom He will": "While I live I hope."

ENTRANCE DOOR, PEFFER MILL.

The date 1636 appears above a dormer window, and

DORMER WINDOW.

sun-dials are to be seen on both the front and back of the house. The thickness of the walls shows the general desire for security at that time, and clearly

SUN-DIAL.

indicates the characteristics of the 17th century. In recent years the aspect of affairs has greatly changed at Peffer Mill. The mill lade, and along with it the dam, with the swans proudly swimming on its surface, have disappeared, and the iron wheel, now rusty and uncared for, has long since ceased to revolve. A century ago a bleachfield for gauze and thread existed at Peffer Mill, which employed a great many hands. A public-house was also near there in 1728, as we know from the following strange circumstance. In that year a woman named Maggie Dickson was hanged in Edinburgh. Her friends, in conveying her body in a cart back to Musselburgh, to which place she belonged, called at the public-house in question to get a "dram," doubtless considering that the eerie character of their

PEFFER MILL HOUSE.

mission rendered it necessary. How long they remained in the tavern is not recorded, but on their return to the cart they were horrified to discover Maggie sitting up in her coffin, the lid of which had not been fastened. She quite recovered, and for the remainder of her life was known by the sobriquet of "Half-hangit Maggie Dickson." Though the public-house, with the gauze and thread works, have been long since swept away, the Suburban Railway with the "iron horse" has wrought wonders, and the grounds around Peffer Mill bid fair at no distant date to be covered with houses and public works.

Between Peffer Mill and Bridgend are the "Craigmillar Irrigated Meadows," intersected by the Suburban Railway. Formerly they were called "the King's Meadows," and there is still extant a charter by King James V., dated at Kirkcaldy, September 2, 1536, whereby he "dimits" to his friend and barber, John Murray, the lands called King's Meadows. This was a favourite hunting-ground of the king, being in the centre of the forest of Drumselch. At that period large areas were covered with immense forests of trees, while others were moor and waste lands. Drumselch forest was then the habitat of large herds of red deer, many of them growing to an immense size. The Rev. Mr White, in his 'History of the Parish of Liberton,' states that Easter Duddingston, which originally belonged to the monastery of Kelso, had a servitude

BRIDGEND FROM THE SUBURBAN RAILWAY.

on the lands of Cameron for peats. It may be mentioned that when excavations were being made in 1887 for the Powburn sewer, on the road running eastwards from Cameron Toll, a thick layer of moss was cut through. On its being dug out, cartloads were taken away by nurserymen, it being deemed invaluable for planting rhododendrons. Embedded in the moss was discovered a number of the antlers of red deer in a wonderful state of preservation. From their large size they contrasted strangely with the antlered heads which are nowadays found in the Highlands of Scotland.

At Bridgend a hunting-lodge was built by James V.,—the initials of his name, the arms of Scotland, and between them the sketch of a huge edifice, all cut in stone, being placed above the gateway. All traces of the hunting-lodge have disappeared, except the stone referred to, which is built into the garden wall at The Inch, and carefully preserved by the present proprietor. A handsome chapel was also built at Bridgend by this pious king, but no vestiges of it remain. In the valuation proceedings before the Commissioner of Teinds in 1630, the lands of Bridgend are called "the Lady Bridgend," which indicates that the chapel there was dedicated to the Virgin, "Our Lady."

PRESTONFIELD.—North from the irrigated meadows

referred to are the house and policies of Prestonfield, the property of Sir Robert Dick Cunninghame, whose family is of very ancient origin. Formerly it was called Priestfield, and in 1681 belonged to Sir James Dick, who was Lord Provost of Edinburgh. While

PRESTONFIELD, FROM ARTHUR'S SEAT.

presiding at a meeting of the Magistrates on 11th Jan. of that year, at eight o'clock in the evening, his house was set on fire by the students of Edinburgh. The Provost, it appeared, had displeased them for not giving them encouragement in burning the Pope's effigy, and in revenge they burnt his house. For this act the College gates were shut, and the students banished fifteen miles from Edinburgh. The Corporation and the Government wished to rebuild the house, but in consequence of the state of the treasury, £800 was all Sir James ever received; and his salary of £200 a-year, as Provost, during the two years he was in office, was never paid. The present mansion was built in 1687. Priestfield was purchased by Sir James Dick from Sir Thomas Hamilton. Sir James subsequently bought land from Preston of Craigmillar, and afterwards called his estate Prestonfield. At one time Prestonfield was covered with oaks, but Sir Thomas Dick Lauder informs us that every possible encouragement to cut them down was held out by the authorities, seeing that it served as a place of shelter "for all manner of thieves and lymmers." When Sir James Dick was Lord Provost of Edinburgh he cleaned the streets at his own expense, and had the refuse carried on the backs of horses to Prestonfield. He at the same time divided and fenced the parks, and as the consequence they grew the richest grass in the country.

NIDDRIE.—Within a distance of two miles from the sea at Portobello is to be seen nestling among the trees the mansion-house of Niddrie. This is the

NIDDRIE HOUSE.

residence of Colonel Wauchope of the Black Watch, his family being the oldest in the county. Robert Wauchope of Niddrie Marischall built a tomb in 1387, on which his name is inscribed; and it is generally supposed that this laird built the chapel also, dedicated to the Virgin Mary in 1389, the revenues of which were attached to Liberton Church at the Reformation. Gilbert Wauchope had a charter of Niddrie from King Robert III., and in 1479 the name of Patrick Wauchope is recorded. Gilbert Wauchope was a member of Parliament in 1560. Robert Wauchope, and Archibald his son, aided and abetted the turbulent Earl of Bothwell in his treasonable and lawless proceedings. On the night of the 12th May 1589, while Archibald Wauchope was lying in Robert Peacock's house at Bridgend, waiting for the Laird of Edmonstone, he was beset by the latter, and an alarm being raised, all Edinburgh was roused. The king came to the Boroughmoor, and directed a herald to charge Wauchope to surrender, under pain of treason. He obeyed the summons, and was committed prisoner to the Tolbooth in Edinburgh. Next day he was brought to trial for the slaughter of the Laird of Sheriffhall and his brother, John Gifford. The trial was continued till late at night, and Wauchope escaped out of the window of the Tolbooth while the judge was still sitting on the bench. Archibald Wauchope must have been a turbulent and determined character, as in Calderwood's History it is stated that during the king's absence in Denmark in 1590, the young laird of Niddrie killed a gentleman dependent of the Abbot of Holyroodhouse, because he reproved him for striking an officer of arms. His death was in keeping with the checkered character of his life. On June 18, 1597, while in concealment in Scletter's Close, Edinburgh, his servant gave the alarm that the Laird of Edmonstone, with a large number of followers, had surrounded the house. Rather than be taken prisoner, Wauchope tried to escape by leaping from a window, but in falling broke his neck.

Colonel Wauchope is the seventeenth laird in direct succession. At an early age he entered on a military career, and served in the Ashantee war of 1873-74 as a special service officer. He was twice wounded, once slightly and once severely, and was honoured with a medal and clasp, besides being mentioned in despatches. From 1878 to 1880 he was appointed Civil Commissioner in Cyprus, and during that time was delegate on the Sultan's Lands Commission, for which he received the title of C.M.G. In the Egyptian expedition in 1882 he took a part, and was present at the battle of Tel-el-Kebir, for which he received a medal with clasp and the Khedive's star. He served in the Soudan expedition under Sir Gerald Graham in 1884 as Deputy Assistant Adjutant and Quartermaster-General, and was in the engagement at El Teb, where he was severely wounded. Again he was honoured with two clasps and being mentioned in despatches. With the first battalion of the Black Watch he served in the Nile expedition in 1884-85, and with the River Column under Major-General Earle took part in the engagement at Kirbekan, where he was very severely wounded, for a time his life being despaired of. He however recovered, and was again presented with a medal and two clasps.

In 1892 Colonel Wauchope contested Mid-Lothian against Mr Gladstone; and though his success was regarded as almost impossible, he succeeded in reducing the majority gained at the previous election by nearly four thousand votes.

The grounds of Niddrie are beautifully and tastefully laid out. At the last addition to the house, Hugh Miller wrought as a stone-mason. "In the walk south of the house," he writes in 'My Schools and Schoolmasters,' "I have enjoyed many an agreeable saunter; and through its long vista I could see the sun sink over the picturesque ruins of Craigmillar Castle." Near to the house, on the road to Musselburgh, is the small village of Niddrie Mill. At one time it was situated on both sides of the rivulet, and contained a great many inhabitants. In it there were three breweries and fourteen public-houses, which are all long since swept away. New breweries, however, on an extensive scale, have recently been erected at Cairntows, about half a mile farther west, in close proximity to Craigmillar railway station.

EDMONSTONE.—Stretching away inland about a mile to the south is to be seen Edmonstone House, which looks down from an eminence, where it is surrounded by some of the finest trees in the country.

Edmonstone House is the residence of Sir John Don Wauchope, the descendant of one of the most promi-

EDMONSTONE HOUSE, FROM CRAIGMILLAR WOODS.

nent families in Mid-Lothian. The building has a modern appearance, but portions of it are known to be at least four hundred years old. At the close of the last century it was partially burnt, and on being restored, considerable alterations were made. On the workmen breaking out a window in the room now occupied as the library, a skeleton of a man was discovered, who doubtless had been entombed centuries before. It was surmised he might be one of the Wauchopes of Niddrie, captured in one of the numerous fights between the two families of Wauchope of Niddrie and the Edmonstones at that period. It appeared that a feud had broken out between them in the reign of James V. which became hereditary, and was kept up for a century. On the skeleton being taken out, the shoes appeared to be perfect, but, on being exposed to the air, they crumbled into dust. A sword was found beside the skeleton, which, unfortunately, has not been preserved.

The Edmonstones of that ilk sold the property to James Rait in 1626, whose grand-daughter and heiress married John Wauchope, a younger son of the Laird of Niddrie. When this John Wauchope was christened, in 1633, King Charles I. happened to be present, and took from his neck a gold, pearls, and blue enamel chain, which he put round the neck of the child, and which is now highly treasured as an heirloom in the Wauchope of Edmonstone family.

LITTLE FRANCE. — Within a short distance of Edmonstone lies Little France, consisting of a few small houses which can scarcely with propriety be designated a village. This spot is specially rich in historical interest, and gets its name from the French retainers of Queen Mary residing there when she held her court at Craigmillar Castle. Within recent years there stood at the west side of the road a small thatched cottage which tradition asserted to be a remnant of the original village of Little France. In corroboration of this tradition, it may be mentioned that an oak lintel above the door had some words inscribed upon it in the French language. On the cottage becoming tenantless it was maliciously set on fire, so that this interesting relic of bygone days was completely destroyed. It is here, as observed in a previous chapter, that the venerable sycamore known as "Queen Mary's Tree" has braved the storms of so many generations.

KINGSTON GRANGE.—Adjoining Little France is the estate and mansion of Kingston Grange. This property has been added to the estate of Craigmillar by its having been purchased by the present proprietor, Captain Gordon Gilmour. Formerly it was called Sunnyside, but the name was changed when it was purchased by the late Mr Hay, of Duns Castle, to perpetuate the memory of his ancestor, Viscount Kingston. At the east side of the park are some cottages which still bear the name of Sunnyside. The park, which is eighty acres in extent, and beautifully furnished, is a feu off the barony of Moredun.

MOREDUN.—The house and estate of Moredun, formerly called Goodtrees, is of considerable antiquity, and in olden times belonged to the Herries family—a family of much local influence in the fourteenth and fifteenth centuries. It afterwards became the property of Lord Somerville, along with the estate of Drum and half of the estate of Gilmerton. There-

KINGSTON GRANGE.

after it was possessed by the Macullochs; and through the marriage of Marion, only daughter and heiress of David Maculloch, with Sir James Stewart of Coltness and Kirkfield, it eventually became the property of the Stewarts, in whose hands it remained till 1775.

MOREDUN HOUSE.

Sir James Stewart was an Edinburgh merchant, and at one time Lord Provost of the city. He took the side of the Covenanters in 1661, and, as indicated in a previous chapter, his house of Goodtrees was on one occasion searched by a party of dragoons sent out from Edinburgh to apprehend Hugh M'Kail, who had been at first tutor and then chaplain in Sir James's family. His son, also Sir James, was still more distinguished. His faithful adherence to the Stuart family forced him, like his royal masters, to live for many years in exile. After the Revolution he returned home, obtained a complete pardon, and became afterwards Lord Advocate for Scotland.

In 1775 Goodtrees was purchased by Mr Mackenzie of Delvine, who sold it in 1769 to Baron Stewart Moncrieff, and while in the occupancy of this gentleman the name of Goodtrees was changed, under a royal charter, to that of Moredun. At the beginning of the present century Moredun was bought by Mr Samuel Anderson, by whom, and afterwards by his son, Mr David Anderson, banker in Edinburgh, it was possessed until 1888, when it was purchased by the present proprietor, Mr John Welsh, who has restored and improved the house, in harmony with its original character and surroundings. Mr David Anderson was long a Director of Fettes College, and took an active interest in that well-known educational institution.

The mansion-house of Moredun is situated in a beautifully wooded park, and fronts the north-west—Liberton Church, Craigmillar Castle, and the distant

VIEW IN MOREDUN PARK.

spires of the city being seen over its surrounding trees. The policy at the west side is intersected by a winding rivulet, over which are some picturesque rustic bridges, and on both sides are many charming walks through the pleasure-grounds. This wooded dell reminds one forcibly of Hawthornden, and its sylvan beauties form the subject of many an artist's canvas. From 1760 to 1785 the garden at Moredun claimed pre-eminence as being the richest in the county; and it was believed to be the first in which forcing was carried out to any degree of perfection. Baron Moncrieff, the proprietor, used to boast that from his own ground, within a few miles of Edinburgh, he could, by the aid of glass, coals, and a good gardener, match any country in Europe in peaches, grapes, pines, and every other fine fruit excepting apples and pears. These, he acknowledged, were grown better in the open air in England and the north of France. James Boswell, the biographer of Dr Johnson, was on intimate terms with Baron Moncrieff, and was a frequent visitor at Moredun. On one occasion, when Boswell was narrating his frolics over his success in the great Douglas cause, Moncrieff said to him, "By my soul, Boswell, you're mad!" to which he replied, glibly and cuttingly, "Swear by your peach-houses, your pineries, and your vineries at Moredun, but by nothing so worthless as your soul!"

It is not generally known that Moredun was called after the hill of that name on the Moncrieff estate at Perth, Baron Moncrieff being a scion of that family. In the charter-chest and library there are some rare MSS. of great antiquarian and historical interest.

STENHOUSE.—Contiguous to the grounds of Moredun is the hamlet of Stenhouse, which is picturesquely situated in the wooded glen through which flows the Burdiehouse burn. This hamlet appears at one time to have been larger than it is now, though a century ago the inhabitants numbered only 175. There is little history of an interesting character associated with it, except that it is the birthplace of John Simpson, the celebrated architect, whose remains lie interred in the new church of St Chad, at Shrewsbury. He was architect for the bridges of Bewdley, Dunkeld, and Bonar, the aqueducts of Pontoysclite and Chirk, the locks and basins of the Caledonian Canal, and the church of St Chad, in which he is now interred. It may be also mentioned that Bessie Lecost and other four women belonging to this place were con-

STENHOUSE.

victed of witchcraft, by their own confession, and were strangled and burnt. They were called "the Stenhouse witches."[1] Stenhouse is also memorable for its connection with the famous, or rather infamous, Grizzel Sempill, generally known as Lady Gilton or Jelton. She was the wife of Sir James Hamilton of

HYVOT'S MILL.

Stenhouse, Provost of Edinburgh. According to Buchanan, this woman was taken away from her

[1] Lord Roystoun's MSS.; Abstract of Justiciary Records in Moredun Library.

husband by Archbishop Hamilton, who "kept her as if she had been his lawful wife, though she was remarkable neither for beauty nor reputation, nor indeed for anything but wantonness." She bore three children to the Archbishop.[1] Calderwood, Knox, and other historians of the time, also make mention of Lady Gilton.

The walk between Stenhouse and Gilmerton is very picturesque. The neighbourhood is frequently visited by artists, and sketches of parts of it are often reproduced on canvas. Hyvot's Mill stands about half way between the two places.

GILMERTON.—Almost south of Craigmillar Castle may be seen the village of Gilmerton. Prior to the introduction of railways, the population of Gilmerton, in common with other suburban villages, consisted chiefly of carters, who daily conveyed coal and other commodities into Edinburgh. Within the memory of many persons still living, it was no uncommon thing to find the family and the horse under the same roof. This state of matters, however, has disappeared

[1] Buchanan, ' Rer. Scot. Hist.,' Book xv., chap. 65.

before the advance of sanitary science. The inhabitants of Gilmerton have long had the reputation of being lawless and disorderly. This, however, does not comport with our experience. Having had occasion to pass through the village at all hours of

GILMERTON HOUSE.

the day and night, we never met with anything but the greatest courtesy and civility.

Among places of interest at Gilmerton is Gilmerton House, which was the dower-house of the ladies of

Newbyth, the property of Gilmerton belonging to Sir David Baird of Newbyth. Gilmerton House is now tenanted by miners, and is rapidly losing its ancient character. "The mansion-house," says the Rev. Mr White, who wrote over a century ago, "has a

GILMERTON, LOOKING EAST.

most excellent site, and is favoured with a most charming and delightful prospect on all hands. The like is hardly to be seen anywhere. What is called the long walk on the south side of the house is peculiarly pleasant. At the east end of it there is a large arch, and above it a balcony in order to enlarge and improve the view."

On entering the village, going towards Dalkeith, the first thing that meets the eye is the announcement regarding the "Gilmerton subterranean cave." This cave was long considered a great curiosity, and was visited by people from all parts of the country. It is still shown to the public, and well repays inspection. It is said to have been hewn out of the solid rock by a blacksmith named George Paterson, who, after five years' hard work, finished it in 1724. There he lived with his family, and conducted his business as a blacksmith till his death in 1735. Pennycuick, the poet, left an inscription on it to the following effect :—

> " Upon the earth thrives villainy and woe,
> But happiness and I do dwell below :
> My hands hew'd out this rock into a cell,
> Wherein from din of life I safely dwell :
> On Jacob's pillow nightly lies my head,—
> My house when living, and my grave when dead.
> Inscribe upon it, when I'm dead and gone,
> ' I liv'd and died within my mother's womb. ' "

In the reign of David II. the barony of Gilmerton

belonged to Sir John Herries, who had a beautiful daughter. This young lady was inclined to be melancholy, and appeared to be very strict in observing all the religious rites and ceremonies then in use. A young Cistercian monk from the richly endowed Abbey of Newbattle insinuated himself into her favour under the pretext of holiness,—" but this rascal, by his divellish rhetoric and allurements, soe far prevailed upon the simplicitie of this gentlewoman that at length he betrayed her."[1] Sir John discovered his daughter's guilt, and learned that intercourse was carried on at Gilmerton Grange through the connivance of the lady's nurse, who at this time was a widow, and resided there. Being a passionate man, Sir John threatened his daughter with death if ever it came to his knowledge that she again frequented the Grange. On a dark windy night he discovered that the objects of his vengeance were engaged in a stolen interview, and, accompanied by two of his servants, he repaired to the Grange and demanded admittance. Notwithstanding his threatenings, they made no answer to

[1] 'Memory of the Somervilles.'

GILMERTON CAVE.

his demands, and in a fit of rage he seized a torch from one of his servants and set fire to the thatch. As a high wind was blowing, the house was speedily reduced to ashes, all the occupants, including the young lady Margaret Herries, perishing in the flames. The place was thereafter called Burntdool or Burndale. The exact spot where the tragedy took place is not known, but the gamekeeper's house at Melville is called Burndale Cottage to this day.

DRUM.—A little to the east of Gilmerton stands the historical house of Drum. Situated on rising ground, the surrounding trees are distinctly seen from Craigmillar. Built originally by Hugh seventh Lord Somerville in 1585, it was long regarded as a venerable building. Shortly after completion it was burnt down, was anew rebuilt, and in 1629 was again burnt, being this time left for more than a century in ruins. Between 1730 and 1740 James thirteenth Lord Somerville pulled down what remained, and built the house as it at present stands, the stones from the ancient edifice being utilised in the construction of the new one. Formerly the barony of Drum belonged to the Herries family, but it eventually came into the possession of the Somervilles, through Sir Walter de Somerville marrying, in 1375, Giles, only surviving daughter and heiress of Sir John

DRUM HOUSE.

Herries, and sister of Margaret, who, as already mentioned, so unhappily perished in the Burndale tragedy.

"Drum" signifies the ridge of a hill, and from

here the celebrated forest of Drumselch — Gaelic, *druim sealche*, i.e. *the hill of the hunting* — extended almost to Holyrood.

In Lord Somerville's time it was regarded as

DRUM HOUSE, FROM THE SOUTH-EAST.

the most beautiful place in Mid-Lothian, what is still called the deer-park being tastefully laid out in shrubberies. Lord Somerville sold the Drum to Mr Hay, who worked the coal, and in a great measure destroyed it as a residence. It then passed into the possession of Robert Cathcart, W.S. Mr Cathcart's trustees subsequently sold the house and policy to Mr Gilbert Innes of Stow. Mr Innes was unmarried, and was succeeded by his sister, at whose death the Drum passed to Mr Alexander Mitchell, from whom it was purchased by the present proprietor, Mr More Nisbet.

Craigmillar and its environs, it will thus be seen, are rich and varied in historical associations, as well as in agricultural and mineral wealth. And to these must be added those general features of the far-reaching landscape which have been the admiration of so many successive generations. Here Sir Walter Scott received some of his finest inspirations; and here many of the cultured and refined of a past age, in the palmy days of Scotland's capital, were wont to linger oft, and dwell fondly on the scene spread out before their eyes. They have all passed away, but the landscape remains, lovely as of yore. And here we too would now fain pause, while memory recalls the " storied lore " which the scene evokes.

INDEX.

Amphibia of Craigmillar district, the, 73 *et seq.*
Andersons of Moredun, the, 228.
Aquatic fowl, the, of Duddingston Loch, 81 *et seq. passim.*
Architectural features, the, of Craigmillar Castle, 1 *et seq.*
Armorial bearings, ancient, at Craigmillar Castle, 21 *et seq.*
"Arthur's Seat fern," the, 135.
Arthur's Seat, flora of, 125, 132, 143 *et seq.*—examples of glacial action at, 161.
Avifauna of Craigmillar district, the, 80 *et seq.*

Badger, the, in Craigmillar district, 54.
Balcanquall, Walter, 185.
Balm Well, the, 195.
Barn owl, the, 85.
Bat, the, 62—Daubenton's, nest of, at The Inch, *ib.*
Binning, John, executed for murder of Darnley, 40.
Bird-life, the, of Craigmillar district, 80 *et seq.*
Black-backed gull, the great, 111.
Blackbird, the, 101.
Blackcap, the, 118.
Blackford Hill, 177—National Scottish Observatory at, *ib.*
Black-headed gull, the, 111.
Blind-worm, the, at Craigmillar, 71 —on the Braids, 72.
Blue tit, the, 116.
Boroughmoor, the, 176.
Botany of the Craigmillar district, 124 *et seq.*
Bothwell, 1st Earl of, conference at Craigmillar attended by, 36— marriage of, to Queen Mary, 39 —testament of, 40.
Bothwell, 2d Earl of, battle fought near Craigmillar by troops of, 42 *et seq.*
Braids, the, 192—view from, 193.
Bridgend, hunting-lodge of James V. at, 215—chapel at, *ib.*
Bullfinch, the, 122.
Bunting, the snow-, 120—the reed-, *ib.*—the corn-, *ib.*
Burdiehouse limestone, the, 155— fossil remains of, 159.
Burdiehouse, the village of, 196.
Butler, Reuben, supposed residence of, 178.
Buzzard, the, 104.

Carboniferous rocks, the, of Craigmillar district, 156 *et seq.*—fossil remains of, 159.
Carrion crow, the, 89.
Chaffinch, the, 121.
Chapel at Craigmillar Castle, ruins of, 20.
Chiffchaff, the, 118.
Clydesdale, the Winrams of, 170.
Cock-fights, annual, at Liberton parish-school, 178 *et seq.*
Cole tit, the, 116.
Corn-bunting, the, 120.
"Confessional," the, at Craigmillar Castle, 18.
Corn-crake or landrail, the, 102.
Covenanters, defeat of the, at Rullion Green, 197.
Craigmillar, barony of, tenure of the, 30—purchase of, by Sir John Gilmour, 44.

Index.

Craigmillar Castle, architectural features of, 1 et seq.—view from, 1, 31, 168 — keep at, 2, 11 — ground-plan of, 3—doorway of, 4—Great Hall of, 6—Queen Mary's room in, 7—roof of, 10—repairs on, ib.—human skeleton found in dungeon of, 13—towers of, 16—latest addition to, 17 — fish-pond at, 19—ruined chapel at, 20—armorial bearings on walls of, 21—historical associations of, 24 et seq.—earliest records of, 25—early possessors of, ib. et seq.—seizure of, by the English, 34—connection of, with Queen Mary, 35 et seq.—conference at, 36—James VI. at, 41—battle at, 42—purchase of, by Sir John Gilmour, 44—last tenants of, 52—"scorpions" at, 71—plants found at, 129 et seq., 143 et seq.
"Craigmillar conference," the, 36.
Craigmillar, derivation of name of, 24—variations in spelling of, 25—environs of, 168 et seq.
Craigmillar district, fauna of, 54 et seq.—avifauna of, 80 et seq.—botany of, 124 et seq.—geology of, 152 et seq.
Craigmillar Irrigated Meadows, the, 213.
Craigmillar sandstone, buildings constructed of, 164 et seq.—superiority of, 165.
"Craigmillar Sycamore," the, 138 et seq.—seedlings from, 140 et seq.
Craigmillar, the Prestons of, 26.
Crake, the spotted, 103.
Cromwell, army of, encamped at Craigmillar, 172—at Galach-law, 194—sword of, at The Inch, 173.
Crossbill, the, 122.
Cuckoo, the, 90—story of a, 91.
Curlew, the, 85.

Dabchick or little grebe, the, 103.
Dalkeith coal-field, the, fossil remains of, 161.
Dalmahoys, the, 182 et seq.
Darnley, proposed divorce of Queen Mary from, 36—plot regarding murder of, 37—perpetrators of the murder of, 39 et seq.
Daubenton's bat, nest of, at The Inch, 62.
Dick, Sir James, of Prestonfield, 217.
Dovecot, the, at Nether Liberton, 175.
Drum, the house of, 239—successive proprietors of the barony of, ib.
Drumselch, the ancient forest of, 213, 241—antlers of red deer found at, 215.
Duck, the long-tailed, 82 — the tufted, ib.—the golden-eye, 83—the scaup, ib.
Duddingston Loch, aquatic fowl of, 81 et seq. passim—plants at, 135 et seq., 143 et seq.—filthy state of, 208—proposed plan for purifying of, ib.—antiquarian "finds" at, 209.
Duddingston, village of, 206—Prince Charlie at, ib.—house of, 207—parish church of, 209.
Dumbiedykes, the Laird of, supposed residence of, 211.

Easter Duddingston Lodge, house and grounds of, 210.
Edinburgh University, books bequeathed to, by Clement Little, 184—Prestonfield House burnt by students of, 216.
Edmonstone House, 222—human skeleton found at, 224.
Edmonstones of that ilk, the, 224.
Environs of Craigmillar, the, 168 et seq.
Ermine fur of commerce, the, 60.

Falcon, the peregrine, 103.
Fauna of Craigmillar district, the, 54 et seq.
Female offenders, novel mode of punishment of, 165.
Fieldfare, the, 101.
Field mouse, the long-tailed, 71.
Fish of Craigmillar district, the, 78.
Fish-pond at Craigmillar Castle, remains of, 19.
Flora of Craigmillar district, vari-

ety of, 124—lists of, already published, 125 et seq.—examples of, 128 et seq.
Fossils, the, of Craigmillar district, 158 et seq.
Fox, the, 56—a hunt of, 57.
French retainers, the, of Queen Mary, at Burdiehouse, 196—at Little France, 225.
Frog, the, 75—fishing with a, 76.

Galach-law, Cromwell's army encamped at, 194.
Garden warbler, the, 118.
Geological features, the, of Craigmillar district, 152 et seq.
Gilmerton Grange, the tragedy of, 238.
Gilmerton House, 235.
Gilmerton Limestone, fossil remains of, 161.
Gilmerton, village of, 234—subterranean cave at, 237.
Gilmour, Captain Wolrige Gordon, biographical notice of, 52—military career of, ib.—alterations on Inch House by, 173.
Gilmour, first Sir Alexander, 48—second Sir Alexander, 49.
Gilmour, Sir Charles, 49.
Gilmour, Sir John, biographical notice of, 44 et seq.—alterations on Craigmillar Castle by, 47.
Gilmour, Walter James Little, 50—career and character of, ib. et seq.—repairs on Craigmillar Castle by, 7, 10, 51.
Gilmour, Walter Little, 50.
Gilmour, Wm. Charles Little. See Little, Wm. Charles.
Gilmour, Wm. Little, of Liberton and Craigmillar, 49—descendants of, 50.
Gilton, Lady, 233.
Glacial action, examples of, in Craigmillar district, 161 et seq.
Goatsucker or night-jar, the, 103.
Gold crest, the, 116.
Golden plover, the, 109.
Goldfinch, the, 122.
Goodtrees. See Moredun.

Gordon, Robert Wolrige. See Gilmour, Capt. Wolrige Gordon.
Great tit, the, 116.
Grebe, the little, 103.
Greenfinch, the, 120.
Greylag goose, the, 109.
Grey wagtail, the, 119.
Grouse, 109.
Gull, the black-headed, 111—the common, ib.—the great black-backed, ib.—the herring, 112.
Guthrie, Dr, and industrial schools, 181.

"Half-hangit Maggie Dickson," story of, 212.
Hamilton of Bothwellhaugh, Old Woodhouselee owned by, 200—wrong done to, by the Regent Murray, 201—assassination of the Regent by, ib.
Hare, the, 64—a hunt of, at Craigmillar, ib. et seq.
Hedgehog, the, 58—habits of, ib.
Hedge-sparrow, the, 120.
Heron, the, 89.
Herries, Sir John, of Gilmerton, 238.
Herring gull, the, 112.
Hertford, Earl of, attack on Craigmillar Castle by troops of, 34.
Historical associations of Craigmillar Castle, the, 24 et seq.
House-martin, the, 116.
House-sparrow, the, 120.
Hyvot's Mill, 234.

Igneous rocks, the, of Craigmillar district, 157.
Inch House, the, description of, 168—early proprietors of, 170—Cromwell's sword at, 173.
Inch, The, old cottages at, 173.
Industrial School at Liberton, the, 180.
Irrigation-farm at Craigmillar, the, 66—number of rats at, ib.

Jackdaw, the, 89.
Jacksnipe, the, 102.
"Jacky," the Liberton Magpie, 94.
James V., residence of, at Craig-

millar, 34—hunting-lodge of, at Bridgend, 215.
James VI., residence of, at Craigmillar, 41.
Jelton, Lady. *See* Lady Gilton.
Jougs, the, at Duddingston parish church, 209.

Keep of Craigmillar Castle, the, 2, 11.
Kingfisher, the, 84.
King's Meadows. *See* Craigmillar Irrigated Meadows.
Kingston Grange, 226—old cottages at, *ib.*
Kirk-of-Field, murder of Darnley at, 38.

Landrail or corn-crake, the, 102.
Lapwing, the, 109—popular prejudice regarding, 110.
Lark, the, 107— snaring of, *ib.*
Liberton House, 186—antiquarian interest of, 187—restoration of, 188.
Liberton, Lord, 171.
"Liberton magpie," the, 94.
Liberton, Over, barony of, 178 *et seq.*
Liberton, the Winrams of, 170.
Liberton Tower, 190—architectural features of, *ib.*
Liberton, village of, 178—annual cock-fights at parish school of, *ib.*—Industrial School at, 180.
Linlithgow Palace, seedling from Queen Mary's tree planted at, 141.
Linnet, the, 121.
Little, Clement, books bequeathed to Edinburgh University by, 184.
Little, William, of Liberton, 49.
Little, William, Lord Provost of Edinburgh, 185.
Little, William Charles, of Liberton, 49—surname of Gilmour assumed by, 50.
Little, William Rankine. *See* Rankine, William.
Littles, family of the, 184 *et seq.*
Little France, hamlet of, 225—Queen Mary's tree at, 138 *et seq.*, 226.
Lizards, 73.
Long-eared owl, the, 88.
Long-tailed tit, the, 116.

Magpie, the, 94—"The Liberton magpie," *ib.*
Mallard duck, the, 80.
Mar, Earl of, imprisoned at Craigmillar Castle, 32.
Martin, the sand-, 115—the house-, 116.
Mary, Queen, room of, at Craigmillar Castle, 7 — residence of, at, 35—conference between, and nobles at, 36—marriage of, to Bothwell, 39—alleged connection of, with Darnley's murder, 41—sycamore tree named after, 138 *et seq.*—solitaire and watch of, at Woodhouselee, 204.
Meadow-pipit, the, 120.
Merlin, the, 106.
Mid-Lothian Harriers, "meet" of the, at Craigmillar, 64 *et seq.*
Miller, Hugh, a workman at Niddrie House, 222.
M'Kail, Hugh, at the Pentland rising, 199—execution of, 200.
Missel-thrush, the, 101.
Moncrieff, Baron, of Moredun, 230.
Monteith, Rev. Robert, Episcopal minister of Duddingston, 210.
Moor-hen or water-hen, the, 83.
Moredun, policy of, 226—successive proprietors of, *ib. et seq.*—derivation of name of, 231.
Mortonhall, house and policy of, 194—early proprietors of, 195—the Trotters of, *ib.*
Morton, Regent, executed for murder of Darnley, 40.
Mouse, the long-tailed field, 71—the common, *ib.*
Murray, Regent, treatment of Hamilton of Bothwellhaugh by, 201—assassination of, *ib. et seq.*

National Scottish Observatory, the, at Blackford Hill, 177.

Index.   247

Native plants of Craigmillar district, list of, 143 *et seq.*
Nether Liberton, village of, 174—mill at, *ib.*—dovecot at, 175.
Newts, 73—hatching of, 74.
Niddrie House, 218—grounds of, 222—Hugh Miller a workman at, *ib.*
Niddrie Mill, 222.
Night-jar, the, 103.

Ormiston, Laird of, the confession of, regarding Darnley's murder, 37, 39 *et seq.*
Otter, the, 55—hunt of, at Niddrie, 56.
Over Liberton, barony of, 178 *et seq.*
Owl, the barn, 85—the tawny, 86—the short-eared, 88—the long-eared, *ib.*

Partridge, the, 112.
Paterson, George, excavator of the Gilmerton cave, 237.
Peewit or lapwing, the, 109—popular prejudice regarding, 110.
Peffer Mill, 211—traditionary subterranean passage from Craigmillar to, 14.
Pennycuick, the poet, lines on the Gilmerton cave by, 237.
Pentland Rising, the, 197 *et seq.*
Pentlands, the, 153 *et seq. passim*, 197.
Peregrine falcon, the, 103.
Pheasant, the, 112.
Pied wagtail, the, 119.
Pipit, the tree-, 119—the meadow-, 120—the rock-, *ib.*
Plover, the golden, 109.
Preston, derivation of name of, 26—notices of the family of, *ib. et seq.*—armorial bearings of family of, 16, 21, 27. *See also* St Giles's Cathedral.
Preston, John, and witch-burning, 29.
Preston, Simon or Symon, initials of name of, on Craigmillar Castle, 22—charters of Craigmillar Castle obtained by, 26—children of, 27—royal grants to, 29.

Preston, Sir William de, 26 *et seq.*
Prestonfield, house and grounds of, 216—burning of house of, by students of Edinburgh University, *ib.* — name of, changed from Priestfield, 217.
Proximate landscape of Craigmillar, the, 206 *et seq.*

Quail, the, 83.
Quarries at Craigmillar, notices of the, 164 *et seq.*
Queen Mary. *See* Mary, Queen.

Rankine, William, name of Little assumed by, 189—descendants of, *ib.*
Rats, numbers of, at Craigmillar irrigation-farm, 66.
Redpole, the, 120.
Redstart, the, 122.
Redwing, the, 101.
Reed-bunting, the, 120.
Reptiles at Craigmillar, 71.
Ring-ousel, the, 122.
Robin, the, 117.
Rock-garden, a natural, 133.
Rock-pipit, the, 120.
Rosebery, Earl of, seedling from Queen Mary's tree planted at Linlithgow Palace by, 141.
Rullion Green, battle at, 197—Covenanters' monument at, 198—annual religious service at, *ib.*

Sand-martin, the, 115.
Sandpiper, the common, 122.
Scott Riddell, verses by, in Queen Mary's room at Craigmillar Castle, 8.
Sedge-warbler, the, 117—nest of, *ib.*—song of, *ib.*
Short-eared owl, the, 88.
Shrew, the, 71—the lesser, *ib.*
Silurian System, Upper and Lower, of the Pentlands, fossils of, 158.
Simpson, John, architect, notice of, 231.
Siskin, the, 120.
Slow-worm, the, at Craigmillar, 71—at the Braids, 72.

Index

Snipe, 101.
Snow-bunting, the, 120.
Solitaire, Queen Mary's, at Woodhouselee, 204.
Somerville family, connection of the, with the barony of Drum, 239 *et seq*.
Sparrow-hawk, the, 104—incident of, 105.
Sparrow, the house, 120 — the hedge, *ib*.
Spotted crake, the, 102.
Spotted flycatcher, the, 122.
Squirrel, the, 62.
St Giles's Cathedral, Preston arms in, 27—Preston aisle in, 28.
Starling, the, 113—food of the, 114.
State tragedy, the, at Craigmillar Castle, 31.
Stenhouse, hamlet of, 231.
"Stenhouse witches," the, 231.
Stewart, Sir James, 199, 227.
Sticklebacks as pets, 89.
Stoat, the, 59—skin of the, 60.
Stonechat, the, 123.
Straiton, the village of, 196.
Swallow, the, 115.
Swift, the, 115.

Tawny owl, the, 86 — adventure with a, 87.
Teal, the, 81.
Thomson, Rev. John, parish minister of Duddingston, 210.
Thrush, the, 100.
Tit, the cole, 116—the blue, *ib*.—the great, *ib*.—the long-tailed, *ib*.
Toad, the common, 77.
Tree-creeper, the, 117.
Tree-pipit, the, 119.
Trotters of Mortonhall, the, 195.
Tytler family, eminent men of the, 203.

Upper Liberton, 182—Tower of, 51, 190.

Valleyfield, the Prestons of, 27.
Voles, 67—plague of, 68 *et seq*.

Wagtail, the pied, 119—the white, *ib*.—the grey, *ib*.
Warbler, the sedge-, 117 — the garden-, 118—the wood-, *ib*.—the willow-, 119.
Water-hen, the, 83.
Water-ousel, the, 84.
Water-rail, the, 102.
Wauchope, Col., notice of, 220—Mid-Lothian contested by, 221.
Wauchope, Sir John Don, description of a "run" at Craigmillar by, 57—proprietor of Edmonstone, 222.
Wauchopes of Niddrie, the, 218.
Weasel, the, 59.
Wheatear, the, 123.
Whinchat, the, 123.
Whitethroat, the, 118.
White wagtail, the, 119.
Widgeon, the, 81.
Willow-warbler, the, 119.
Winrams of Clydesdale, the, 170—of Liberton, *ib*.
Witches, trial and burning of, 29—the Stenhouse, 231.
Woodcock, 101.
Woodhouselee, Lord, 203.
Woodhouselee, old mansion-house of, 201—seizure of, by Sir James Bellenden, and its results, *ib. et seq*.—ruins of, 203—present mansion-house of, *ib*.—the Tytlers of, *ib*.—relics of Queen Mary at, 204.
Woodpecker, the great spotted, 97 —story of a, 98 *et seq*.
Wood-pigeon, the, 113.
Wood-warbler, the, 118.
Woolmet, retreat of 2d Earl of Bothwell to, 42, 44.
Wren, the, 117.

Yellowhammer, the, 120.

SECOND EDITION—PRICE FIFTEEN SHILLINGS.

SPORT

IN THE

HIGHLANDS AND LOWLANDS OF SCOTLAND

WITH ROD AND GUN.

BY

TOM SPEEDY.

WITH NUMEROUS ILLUSTRATIONS.

OPINIONS OF THE PRESS.

"The book is sure to have an appreciative multitude of readers among all classes of sportsmen and lovers of natural history."—*Agricultural Journal.*

"His observations are evidently based upon observation which is by no means superficial."—*Inverness Courier.*

"Interesting and comprehensive. . . . . With sportsmen of all kinds its contents will be read with the utmost avidity."—*Perthshire Constitutional.*

"A thoroughly useful and practical book for sportsmen."—*Midland Counties Herald.*

"It gives in excellent style, fresh, vigorous, and limpid as a mountain stream, the experiences of a veteran sportsman, digested, arranged, and made subservient to the purpose of conveying instruction."—*Northern Chronicle.*

"There are few men who could write a work of this kind and add anything fresh to our knowledge of field sports; but Mr Speedy is one of the few."—*Yorkshire Post.*

"Very interesting as well as useful. . . . Mr Speedy possesses considerable descriptive power as well as practical knowledge."—*St James's Gazette.*

"A good practical contribution to sporting literature."—*Athenæum.*

"The volume will be found invaluable. . . . Mr Speedy has a keen eye to nature, and his book gives many interesting lessons in natural history."—*Aberdeen Journal.*

"An unalloyed pleasure."—*Daily Free Press.*

"The writing is lively and fresh. . . The style is almost conversational, and forcibly suggests to the reader the bracken and the heather."—*Southern Reporter.*

"Altogether, Mr Speedy's book is an excellent one."—*North British Daily Mail.*

Opinions of the Press—continued.

"Mr Speedy has a great advantage over many writers of books in that, instead of having to read up his subject, he understands it very well to begin with; his knowledge of it is acquired at first hand."—*Manchester Examiner.*

"An important contribution to the literature of natural history and field sports. . . . The author evidently knows the fauna of Scotland well; while on such subjects as the taking of a moor, dogs, guns, deer, partridge, hare, and ptarmigan, as well as grouse, he has quite a mine of information."—*Liverpool Mercury.*

"A glance at the contents will be sufficient to whet the appetite and to induce perusal. . . . . His chapters on grouse shooting and grouse disease are full of information."—*Glasgow Herald.*

"Mr Speedy's remarks on the breeding ground chosen by grouse show a practical acquaintance with natural history, to acquire a knowledge of which study is among the chief advantages of the sportsman's existence."—*Harper's Monthly Magazine.*

"One of the best books on sporting subjects extant. . . . . There is no part of the natural history connected with sport with which Mr Speedy is not acquainted. . . . It is a delightful book, and one of genuine usefulness."—*Scotsman.*

"Mr Speedy writes pleasantly, and he is eminently practical; and he has had wide experience of the whole range of Scottish sports. . . . We can recommend this volume, with its varied contents, as an admirable handbook to Scottish wild sports."—*Times.*

"The variety of the contents, the thorough knowledge shown of all branches of sport, the fulness of detail, the acquaintance with the habits of the feathered and finny tribes, and the plain common sense shown in every precept and instruction, are evidence of a lifelong study of the subject, and a mastery of each branch of sport in Scotland."—*Standard.*

"Incomparably the best book of the kind. . . Extremely interesting."—*Truth.*

"This book contains many valuable hints."—*The Shooting Times.*

"Mr Speedy writes with a thorough knowledge of his subject, and the book throughout is eminently practical. . . . We recommend it to all our readers."—*Land and Water.*

"'Sport in the Highlands and Lowlands of Scotland' is a delightful volume. . . . . The writer is eminently practical, and has had wide experience in stalking, fishing, and shooting. Mr Speedy, like every true enthusiastic sportsman, is also a naturalist. He has closely studied the habits of beasts and birds, and gives us much entertaining reading on grouse-disease, the habits of the osprey, the cunning of the fox, and many birds of prey. His volume is varied by many personal episodes and exploits, which are always interesting and often exciting.—*Ross-shire Journal.*

WILLIAM BLACKWOOD AND SONS,
EDINBURGH AND LONDON.

www.ingramcontent.com/pod-product-compliance
Lightning Source LLC
Chambersburg PA
CBHW032103220426
43664CB00008B/1118